The
Mickey
Mouse
Trap

The
Mickey
Mouse
Trap · Searching for Applause

by Ron Travisano

ISBN 978-0-578-63802-7

Book design by Philip Travisano
Special thanks to Elizabeth Nader

About The Author

Ron graduated from Pratt Institute in 1960 with a Bachelor of Arts degree, majoring in advertising design.

He began his professional career in 1960 at Young & Rubicam Advertising Agency, starting in the art supply room. Within three years, he worked his way up to an assistant art director.

In 1963 he moved on to Marschalk Advertising where he became an art director, then onto Delahanty, Kurnit and Geller where he became an art supervisor.

In 1966 Ron was mentioned on a front-page story in *The Wall Street Journal* as one of the "Rich Kids" making it big in the advertising world.

In 1967, along with Jerry Della Femina, Ron started his own ad agency, which became one of the best creative agencies in the advertising business throughout the next 18 years.

In 1985 Ron sold his half of the agency back to his partner and started a film production company called Travisano Di Giacomo Films, where he spent the next 18 years producing and directing TV commercials and documentaries.

Ron has won countless awards as an art director, including 15 Clios and several Gold and Silver awards at the "One Show."

As a DGA Film Director, he was awarded both the

Gold and Silver Lions at the Cannes Film Festival for his commercial work.

In 1999 Ron was awarded the Pratt Institute Alumni Achievement Award for professional accomplishment and leadership in communication design.

Ron taught Art Direction classes at Pratt Institute for 12 years, and taught Art Direction at School of Visual Arts for 18 years. He continues to teach Graphic Design at his condo in Cedar Grove, New Jersey.

I dedicate this memoir to
my mother Phyllis,
who trained me in the way to go in life,

my father Biagio,
who always pointed me in a positive direction,

my sister Laura,
who never ceased to inspire me,

my children
Vincent, Philip, Ronnie & Laura
who have been my joy,

and to the memory of
my precious wife Francesca
who I miss more than I can say.

Table of Contents

Part 4

Part 5

Preface

I'm lucky.

I'm so very, very lucky.

I write for a living. So when my friend and partner Ron Travisano asked me to write the forward for this wonderful book, I was honored. Then, of course, I was in a panic.

I wanted so much to repay my friend and to tell the world what he means to me.

What could I say?

How could I say it?

What was the hook?

Everyone who writes knows it's hard to start writing anything unless in the back of your mind you have a hook and you know where you want to go.

As I sat at home in front of my computer … staring … staring… In the background, on my television set, I heard Jimmy Stewart screaming, "Clarence! Clarence!"

Clarence, of course, is an angel who wants his wings, and he's assigned to watch over George Bailey, the Jimmy Stewart character who is a man who wishes he had never been born.

The movie, of course, is *It's a Wonderful Life*. It's everyone's favorite Christmas movie. And then it hit me—I had found my hook.

Come back with me to 1967.

That August, a tiny advertising agency called Jerry Della Femina & Partners, with four equal partners, was born. After only a few months in existence, it was on life support.

We were failing. We had no accounts. We were running out of money. We barely had the next month's rent. Just when I thought it couldn't get any worse—it did.

Ron and I received a letter from our two other partners. They were quitting—leaving us. They had decided it was never going to work. They decided to leave, and they were going off to work at a large agency as a creative team.

Ron and I were stunned. Was this the end?

We took a long walk on the cold streets of New York City and talked. I knew that if Ron left too, I was finished. I couldn't do it alone. I would have to close the agency.

I mumbled and mumbled, and finally, I asked Ron the question, "What are your plans?"

He didn't pause for a second. He looked at me and said, "I will never quit. I'm with you every step of the way."

Twelve words. "I will never quit. I'm with you every step of the way."

That second, Della Femina Travisano & Partners was born.

If Ron hadn't said those words, I have no idea what

my life would be like today. It certainly wouldn't have turned out as wonderfully as it has. I have a pretty good idea that there wouldn't be a house in New York City and another one in the Hamptons, as I have now.

There wouldn't have been a restaurant called "Della Femina" in East Hampton that I owned for 19 years. There would be no gourmet food market. No ownership of *The Independent*, an East Hampton newspaper.

I wouldn't have had any of the things that have made my life so rich and satisfying.

Advertising would never have seen the Ralston Purina Meow Mix "singing cat" (Ron's idea), Joe Isuzu, Air Wick Stick Ups, Dow Ziploc Bags, Blue Nun Wine, WABC Eyewitness News, and a million other wonderful ads written and produced by the best and the brightest in the advertising business.

There wouldn't have been any jobs for thousands of wonderful people, many of whom still say today that working at Della Femina Travisano was "the best job I ever had in my whole life."

There would not have been thousands of homes and rents paid for by the salaries we paid. There would not be years of free health care which we provided for all our employees, their spouses and their children because it was the "right thing to do."

There would not have been a million laughs ... a million life-long friendships.

There would never have been a single warm, wonderful, intimate relationship … some of which lasted just one glorious night, others which are still going strong and will last forever.

I never would have met my wife Judy (we met when she came to interview me when we had the New York Mets advertising account).

So we wouldn't have had two kids, Jessie and J.T., and as of last November, no little grandbaby named Teddy.

Twelve words that Ron Travisano uttered—that changed thousands of lives for the good.

Twelve words that Ron Travisano uttered—that had a great effect on both our lives.

Today, 53 years later, Ron Travisano and Jerry Della Femina know how right Clarence the Angel was when he said,

"It's a Wonderful Life."

- Jerry Della Femina

Introduction

One of the definitions of the word Trap is, "A device or enclosure designed to catch and retain animals, typically by allowing entry but not exit."

As for me and this look-see at my life, this definition comes as close to it as you can get.

It is exactly what happened to my ego the first time I decided to draw a picture and heard the sound of applause. I stepped into the applause, and if there was an exit, I wouldn't have wanted it!

The picture I drew was of Mickey Mouse, and the applause that followed became an elixir, that to this day, still has me searching for it.

With the sound of applause ringing in my ears, what started out as a hobby became my passion and eventually my profession.

Why am I writing this book, someone asked. At 82 years of age, I certainly have had enough applause. It cannot be as simple as that. And it's not!

I have been blessed coming and going… and as the commercial says, "I know a thing or two … because I have seen a thing or two."

That search for applause had its ups and too many downs. There was a time in my life when I thought the more toys I collected, the more fulfilled I would be… that came to an abrupt stop one day when I decided to buy a Jaguar EXE V-12 at lunchtime and demanded to drive it home the same day…and then proceeded to get stuck in the Lincoln Tunnel with a smoking engine!

The universe was beginning to talk to me, and although I didn't like hearing it at first, it became the saving grace for the rest of my life.

I first heard the voice somewhere in the back of my head, and it said in a soft but serious tone, "You are in over your head."

When I graduated from high school, where no one else could draw nearly as well as me, I was treated almost as though I had secret powers. Then I entered Pratt Institute, where everyone could draw as well as me and even better… The little voice entered for the first time, "You are in over your head." You would think that would destroy me, but it had a motivating power to it, and I realized that being in over your head is how you learn to swim.

You would think that someone who liked the sound of applause so much would crawl into a hole some-where … but that challenge actually got my back up and empowered me to greater things than I ever thought possible.

Part 1

Childhood

The day was Sunday, February 4th. The year was 1945. I was 7 years old and excited to be going to Aunt Suzie's house. She was my Godmother, and you could always smell the "gravy" wafting just as soon as you opened the front door to her house. (Tomato sauce in some parts of New Jersey and Brooklyn was called "gravy" for some reason or another.)

Aunt Suzie made the best ravioli this side of Naples, Italy. The first thing I would do when I got there was run into the bedroom to count the ravioli drying out on the bed. Sometimes, if I got there early enough, she would let me help her make them.

She would place dollops of ricotta mixture onto strips of pasta dough, fold it over, and cut the shape of the ravioli out with the rim of a drinking glass. It was my job to put a dimple in the middle of the ravioli with the touch of my pointer finger.

I loved the smell and feel of the uncooked pasta dough, and when she wasn't looking, I would take some of the scraps of dough that were left over and form a little ball that I kept in my pocket until it dried out and lost its viscosity.

My Aunt Suzie was one of my father's sisters. All together there were eight siblings, four boys and four girls. They were all married with children, and when we all got together, which was practically every Sunday, it looked more like a banquet than a Sunday dinner table.

One week it would be ravioli at Aunt Suzie's, next it would be manicotti or pizza at Aunt Florence's, or stuffed shells at our house, or possibly eggplant parmigiana at Aunt Frances's.

Every one of those dishes, however, called for a huge pot of "gravy" to be simmering on the stove, and each dinner would be followed by serving the meat that was used to cook that gravy, like sweet Italian sausage, braciole, meatballs, and a huge chunk of pork that fell apart with the touch of a fork.

They would brown all the meat before putting them into the gravy, and if you were really lucky, you were given a crusty, browned meatball before it went into the pot. It was uncooked on the inside but crunchy and hot on the outside. Awesome!

This particular day my cousins were off in another room playing with a new Christmas gift called *Bombs Away*. It was a game that gave you the opportunity to drop bombs on Germany and Japan with complete accuracy by looking through this mirrored contraption that focused your sights over a ground map. Once you zeroed in on your target, you yelled out "bombs away!" and let this little bomb with a suction-cupped nose go, hoping to hit the desired target. I wonder what the ACLU would say about a *Bombs Away* game today, but that's another story for another day.

Well, while my cousins were busy bombing the crap out of Berlin, I went off into a separate room with a pencil and paper. I had seen one of my older cousins, Danny (we all called him Dannalucci) drawing earlier in the day, and it looked impressive. Although I don't remember having drawn anything before this day, I do remember that I was more interested in looking like my big cousin than I was in actually drawing anything.

I searched through some old comic books looking for something to copy when I saw this picture of Mickey Mouse, or at least what I thought was Mickey Mouse at the time. I don't know how long it took me to draw that picture of Mickey Mouse; all I know is, when I went into the next room to show my parents, aunts, and uncles, they practically dropped their coffee cups.

"Who did this?" my father asked.

"You did this?" my Aunt Geraldine said.

Then there was this deafening silence, followed by resounding applause from all the grown-ups. The applause was so loud that my cousins dropped the *Bombs Away* game and ran into the dining room to see what was going on.

"Ronnie, you are an artist ... a real artist," said my Uncle Paul. I'm not sure I really understood what a "real artist" was, but it didn't sound like it was a bad thing.

"Who helped you with that drawing ... Dannalucci?

… You didn't do that yourself," said my cousin Edith.

One thing about my cousin Edith, you always knew exactly what she thought.

"I did do it," I said sheepishly.

"By yourself?" she quipped.

"Edith, leave him alone," said my cousin Alba, coming to my rescue.

Alba was the one cousin out of the 26 cousins that was born in the same year as I was. It seems that all the cousins were born in sets of twos, and our parents were forever matching us up—Me and Alba, Annamarie and Edith, Laura and Danny, Phyllis and Alex, Robert and Chip, Russell and Dannalucci, and so on.

Edith had a way of boring a hole in my confidence, and I almost began to cry. Aunt Florence, Edith's mom, shot her a look from across the room, and she backed off.

"Yes," I said, regaining my composure. "I did it all by myself." Looking toward my Uncle Paul for support, I blurted out, "I am an artist."

My three big cousins (Danny, Dannalucci, and Russell) pored over my drawing of Mickey like they were art critics from *The New York Times*. They were all pretty good artists in their own right, so it was gratifying to see them each nod their approval.

"Wow! This is great!" I said to myself. "If you draw pictures, people clap and say nice things to you. Well, most of them do anyway."

From that day on I considered myself an artist. I mean, there were plenty of people around me that took pencil to paper, but... I was ... an artist! It was as though my DNA included "artist" as part of its makeup.

It was almost as though I had been knighted or something. "I ... am ... artist!" "You Tarzan ... Me artist!"

Now that I knew I was an artist, there was little else I wanted to do. I drew pictures everywhere and on everything. I started getting notes sent home to my parents that I wasn't listening in class, but was doodling and drawing instead. The teachers reprimanded me for drawing in the borders of books; after all, they were the property of the Kearny School System. The teachers made me stay after school to clean up not only the books that had my handiwork in them but also all the books that were abused by my itchy-fingered fellow students. As an extra punishment, I had to wash all the blackboards and then beat the chalk out of all the erasers outside the doors of the school during the week of the blizzard of '47.

I got so into art that my mother redesigned my bedroom. She had cabinets built-in with an art table in one corner and slats in the cabinets to store my art pads and drawing board. It made me feel even more like an artist. Now I had my own bedroom studio. I must tell you I spent most of my time away from school in that room. I practically lived there.

Outside my bedroom window, I could see my friends playing touch football, step ball, stickball, and dirt bombs. We would take clumped-up, dried chunks of dirt, which was the result of a rainfall, and we'd have wars with each other. We called them dirt bombs because when we threw them, they exploded on impact. We would create the sound effects with our mouths.

I guess bombs were a big thing back then with all the propaganda movies on war that were showing. You could hear Mrs. Bondon yelling out the window, "You kids are going to blind someone… What if there is a stone in one of those things? … and who is going to clean up all this mess?"

Anyway, I would see my friends playing war outside my window, and they would call up to me to come out, but now that I was an artist, I no longer had the time or the desire to throw dirt bombs.

I did, however, continue my escapades with my friends on Mischief Night. For those of you that didn't grow up in New Jersey, that was the night before Halloween when we all went out and caused minor havoc amongst the neighborhood homes.

We thought it great fun to dress the trees in front of the houses with rolls of toilet paper dripping down like tinsel and soaping up the windows of cars that were foolishly left outside. Two of my favorite pranks were *The Dog Poop in the Bag* and *The Invisible Door Knockers*.

The Dog Poop in the Bag was a concept of sheer genius and worked every time. What we did to Mr. Greco was wonderfully wrong. We filled a paper bag with as much dog poop as we could find. In those days there was no such thing as "scooping the poop," so there was always plenty of stock lying around. The more poop in the bag, the better. We put the bag on Mr. Greco's front stoop, lit it on fire, and then rang the bell. I know I don't need to explain to you what happened when he answered the door, but I am sure he must have ended up with dog poop on his socks.

The door-knocker caper wasn't nearly as vicious, but just as much fun. What we did was tie the finest thread to the victim's door-knocker and extend it completely across the street and behind a hedge where we would proceed to pull on the thread without being seen. This would set the door-knocker into action, and the poor soul came to the door to find no one there. We continued the process until it became a game. Door knock, door opened, door knock, door opened. The homeowner heard the knock, jumped on it in an effort to catch the prankster, each time baffled at how anyone could do such a thing and be quick enough to get away before the door was opened.

I guess once creative always creative.

My love for art and the need for the approval that went along with it became intoxicating.

I had an older cousin, well he wasn't exactly my cousin. He was my mother's cousin, who became rather famous in the advertising business. He was what they call an art director or a commercial artist. They are the ones responsible for creating and designing the graphics, typography, artwork, directing the photography, and the retouching for advertisements that eventually end up in a magazine or newspaper.

His name was Vincent DiGiacomo, and he was the first creative director of a very famous advertising agency called Ogilvy, Benson, and Mather. He, along with David Ogilvy, created one of the most memorable symbols in advertising for the Hathaway Shirt Company. They used a rather distinguished English-looking model with grey hair and a black mustache. They placed a black patch over one of his eyes, which was a totally fresh, powerful, and truly unforgettable image.

My mom and I went to visit cousin Vince and his family in New Canaan, Connecticut. Not only was he an accomplished art director, but he was a rather good artist as well. I'll never forget him showing me his studio. The room was behind a hidden wall that somehow turned or slid away, revealing his private hideaway. My eyes must have looked like two sunny-side-up eggs when I walked into that room. The smell of turpentine reminds me of his studio to this day.

He had several used metal coffee cans that held

different sized paintbrushes, canisters filled with pencils, and small boxes with bits of charcoal and Conté Crayons. There were tubes of paint half rolled up and strewn about. On the walls were taped sketches of ideas for future paintings, and in the corner of the room, there was a still life set up of an old and battered bugle lying across an American Flag. There were at least nine or ten stretched canvases of different sizes leaning against the wall, and a large easel that had been splattered with years' worth of painting.

I distinctly remember saying to myself, "This is what an artist studio is supposed to look and smell like... This is what I want to be... This is what I want to do!"

On that first trip to his home, I brought some artwork that I had done. He looked over all of it scrupulously while puffing on a huge Cuban cigar and tugging unconsciously at the strap of his red suspenders. Finally, he looked at my mom and said, "Phyllis, the boy shows great promise." He then looked over at me, squinting through a cloud of smoke, "Ronnie, I see a lot of talent here, but you've got to stay at it if you want to make something of yourself ... There are vultures out there who'll want to eat you up and spew you out when they've gotten everything they can out of you."

I didn't really know what he meant about the vultures and all; I was too excited thinking about his comment of me showing real promise. That's all I could hear, and I guess that's all I wanted to hear!

Now I wasn't exactly sure at the time what he did as a commercial artist in the advertising business. All I knew was—I wanted to be just like him.

I became more and more inquisitive about everything around me. I remember looking at some family photos that my mom always kept in the bottom drawer of the dining room buffet cabinet and thinking, "Gee, my parents grew up in a black and white world. I wonder when color was introduced." I actually thought that color started with my generation.

In 1949 when I was 11 years old, my dad took me to my first baseball game at Yankee Stadium to watch the Yanks play against the Cleveland Indians. Satchel Paige was pitching in one of his last games with the Indians. When I walked into the stadium, my mouth practically dropped to the floor. The stadium was bursting with color. The grass was this brilliant green, the sky blue, the dirt was a bright ochre color, and the stands were filled with colorful flags and banners. I couldn't believe it. Up until then, all I saw of Yankee Stadium was on my black and white Philco TV set seen through this silly magnifying glass.

The Naked Truth

In the early fifties, I began going to Saturday art classes at some school in Newark, New Jersey with a friend of mine by the name of Chuck Mazzeo. I'll never forget our first class. We couldn't have been much more than 13 or 14 at the time, and we were as excited as can be as we climbed the three flights of stairs, awkwardly holding these huge drawing pads under our arms. They were just about long enough to get around the stiff cardboard backings on the pads. I found black and blue marks in my armpits in the shower the next morning. We had to carry these heavy metal fishing tackle boxes that held our drawing equipment as well.

By the time we sat down in the class, we were ready for a nap. We placed the drawing pads on our laps in preparation to draw from live models when this woman came out in this short bathrobe thing. As we fussed with our pads and charcoal pencils, she began to remove her robe. Much to our amazement, she stood before us completely naked! I could feel the blood instantly rush to my head. I am sure my face must have turned a bright shade of red.

Up until now, my knowledge of what naked women looked like was limited to pictures I found in my father's *National Geographic* magazines. I had never seen a naked woman before, and I became incredibly uncomfortable.

The instructor, noticing the looks on our faces, rushed over to the model and whispered something in her ear. She immediately left the room and came back with her robe open, now dressed in a bra and panties.

We went there every Saturday morning hoping to see that woman naked again, but from then on, they made my friend Chuck and me draw from plaster casts of Greek statues and busts of a different kind ... like Voltaire and Julius Caesar.

As the years went on, I began to draw people's faces from photographs in pencil, and I was able to make my drawings look just like them. I especially liked doing portraits of movie stars like Burt Lancaster, Debbie Reynolds, Frank Sinatra, Marlon Brando, and Elvis Presley.

I did this drawing of Tony Curtis, and my mom convinced me to send it to him. Not long after, I got a letter back from him.

It read like this, "Dear Mr. Travisano, The sketch was lovely, and thank you very much. You are a very good artist. I hope you continue doing very well. My very best wishes for a happy holiday! Thanks again. Kindest regards, Tony Curtis."

That was December 18, 1956, and it pumped me up like you can't believe. Now even Tony Curtis knows that I am an artist.

My mom and dad got divorced when I was around

twelve years old, which was highly unusual in those days. My sister Laura, who was six years older than me, was already in college. She went one summer, along with several other girls from her school, on a trip through Europe.

That was a good thing and a bad thing at the same time.

It was good in that she came back with all kinds of information and books about the French impressionist painters that lived around the turn of the century like Degas, Monet, Toulouse-Lautrec, and Renoir. In doing so, she opened up a whole new world of art for me, one that I still am enamored with to this day.

Along with that wonderful discovery, however, came the notion that I should not be allowed to go to Kearny High School.

"I don't think Ronnie should go to Kearny High School," she said to my mother. "He should go to a private school like the young boys do in England."

I thought I would never forgive her for that. She, having gone through the Kearny High School System, thought it better for me to go off to a private school since my father wasn't around as much, and she was off to school in Pennsylvania, and my mom would be going off to work. (By the way, the school my sister went to was an all-girls school called Beaver College. I don't think that name would cut it nowadays!)

"But Mom, all my friends are going to Kearny High

School," I cried.

"I've seen your friends," she said. "Your sister is right."

Carteret Prep

The first year at Carteret Prep in West Orange, New Jersey was spent living at this incredible dormitory high up on a hill with an amazing view of New York City. My eyes welled up with tears as I saw my mom's car winding its way out of the forested property. Although I was only about 10 miles from home, it might as well have been in Ohio for all I cared.

The first person I met was Mr. Hanford A. Farnum, a graduate of Harvard University, and who had done his graduate studies at Oxford to boot. He looked and acted exactly like what you would think a Hanford from Harvard and Oxford would look and sound like.

He was in charge of the dormitory, and he introduced me to the other boys who were checking me out from head to toe. There was Marcus Fuenmayor, Aquiles Rudolfo Benitez, Numa Pompilio Pena Vargas, and his brother Servio Tulio Pena Vargas. They were all rich kids from Venezuela whose parents made it big in the cattle business as well as Pablo Martinez, a famous conductor's son from Barcelona, Spain.

Then there was this nattily dressed senior with slicked-back shiny hair who practically slept in his bowtie. His name was James Todd Thompson. He was from California, and he could tell you anything you wanted to know about any racetrack or horse in the country.

Whenever he could, he would slip off and make his way to Yonkers Raceway, Belmont, or Monmouth Park in South Jersey to place a little bet. One time he disappeared for a few days and finally had to be wired money after an unsuccessful trip to Churchill Downs in Kentucky.

Here I was an artist from Kearny, New Jersey. I could almost see my house from the dormitory window... What in heaven's name was I doing in this school for pampered rich kids?

Luckily I made friends the very next day with this regular kid who lived near the school in West Orange and commuted every day. His name was Matt Palmieri, and I guess we must have looked like brothers or something, because they were forever calling out to us, "Here comes Mike and Ike—they look alike." It was 1953, and that was a takeoff on the presidential campaign theme for Ike Eisenhower.

Matt and I still hold the indoor record for spending time in the bathroom, combing our hair into a perfect DA. That's "Duck's Ass" if you must know.

Although I had a bit of a hard time relating to these kids that were mostly rich rejects from public school, I soon won some favor with my ability to draw, especially from this kid named Erick Friedman.

He used to call me "The Artist."

Erick was an incredibly talented violinist and a

prodigy studying under Jascha Heifetz. He eventually went on to become a rather famous virtuoso.

I remember he used to come to school for a few hours and then go home and practice the violin for eight hours or more. Most of the kids in the school couldn't relate to him, but we had something in common… We both loved to draw.

I first noticed him drawing cars on his note pads, and that became the glue in our friendship. Erick was fascinated with the fact that I could make a drawing of someone and make it look just like the person. In fact, everyone seemed to be impressed—everyone but Mr. Hammond, that is.

Arthur N. Hammond was this little mouse of a teacher with a rather large proboscis, and he took great offense at my cartoon of him that ended up in the school yearbook. He tried to make my life miserable from that day forward. I lost favor with him, but what did I care? It helped me look like a hero with all the guys.

My favorite teacher was a man by the name of Richard A. George. He was born in Wilshire, England, and was an incredible poet and a wonderful teacher. He was the only person who could have made history interesting to me at the age of 15. He didn't believe that history was only about remembering dates and titles of things. He made it real and exciting through art and poetry. Needless to say, he and I got along very well.

When teaching us about World War II, he recalled an actual incident where a dead soldier had been hastily buried, leaving one of his arms sticking out of the dirt grave. It was an eerie image, and he underscored the vision with a wonderful poem.

I remember coming back to school from a weekend with my father. We had gone to the Metropolitan Museum of Art to see some statues by Michelangelo. The one that impressed me the most was one of Moses. I was taken by the way his beard flowed amongst his fingers and that you could actually see the veins underneath the skin in his hands. When I shared the experience with Mr. George, he was impressed with my sensitivity to such a thing.

In 1956 he signed my yearbook and wrote, "Art is all."

The Blessing of Failing at Summer Jobs

My mom wanted me to become a doctor, but I was only interested in one thing... art. I wanted to be a Commercial Artist!

It took a few D's in chemistry and biology to convince her that I was not medical school material. To this day, the only thing I remember from those classes is that "Osmosis is diffusion through a semi-permeable membrane."

It took her a while to get over the idea that I wasn't going to become Ben Casey.

It was my summer jobs that convinced me that I had to, at all costs, get my mom to support my desire to be an artist like her cousin, Vincent DiGiacomo.

One summer, I worked in a factory that rebuilt auto parts for 13 dollars a week, but they let me go not long after they discovered that I was marking boxes of transformers with the wrong code names, and they were all coming back with nasty notes attached to them.

I worked on a Coca-Cola truck for two days before dumping four cases of soda down on my driver, who was six steps below me, opening the back door to the supermarket. I almost killed the poor guy. When I somehow jammed the dolly cart into the truck bin in such a way that we couldn't get it out, he said, "I really think you should look to do something else."

The best one was working at a potato and coleslaw salad company called Gaffney's. The first day I was asked to remove the cores out of a bin full of cabbage heads by drilling them out with a standing drill press.

"Make sure you throw the ones with the worms in the garbage bin and the good ones in the processing bin," said the supervisor. But not unlike Lucille Ball on the chocolate candy line, the cabbage heads kept coming faster and faster, and I was drilling and drilling... totally forgetting which bin was which. I couldn't eat coleslaw for five years after working there.

Then somehow they decided to make me second chef on the potato salad line. We had this huge silver pot with silver blades that kept turning and churning the ingredients. It was so big you needed to use a small stepladder to reach the opening, and we used this silver shovel and silver pitchfork to throw in the potatoes, mayonnaise, and chopped celery. As I was about to throw in a shovel full of potatoes, a moth the size of a Boeing 747 flew into the mixture, and I watched the blades turn and bury the poor thing.

I turned to the chef and said, "I guess we're gonna' have to dump this out."

He made this funny little smirk, chuckled to himself and continued to dump in another silver bucket of mayo. That did it for me for store-bought potato salad as well.

Finally, I told my mom that I wanted to be like her cousin Vince DiGiacomo, and she had to sit down.

"Do you know how rare it is to be a successful artist?" she said. "My cousin is a rare case. Most artists starve to death. Is that what you want?" she went on.

After weeks of interrogation and her testing my resolve to its limits, she finally agreed that I could apply to Pratt Institute in Brooklyn. But only if I agreed to take some teaching courses so that I would have something to fall back on if I didn't succeed as an art director in the advertising business.

There was a mindset that came out of the Depression years that had an entire generation of people looking at every possibility as though it was going to fail.

My mom was one of those overprotective people who, for some reason, took more than a mild interest in my toilet training than I would like to remember. Every morning she would make me breathe in her face and then ask me if I moved my bowels.

Move them? I didn't even know where they were, how could I move them? She would check out my stools, no kidding! She would read them like they were tea leaves or something. "I thought I told you to chew your corn!" she'd yell.

I think she was performing some kind of Voo-Doo-Doo!

In some ways, I think her worrying over my every move acted as fuel for me to press on, so to speak, to succeed at everything and anything I set my mind to.

The one thing I was sure of was my abilities as an artist.

That is until I actually set foot in the hallowed halls of Pratt Institute. Before coming to Pratt, I was an artist set apart from almost everyone around me. Other than my friend Chuck Mazzeo, I never met anyone that could draw as well as I could. Suddenly I was surrounded by hundreds of extremely talented people. They all came from art high schools, like Music and Arts and the School of Industrial Arts. These kids could knock your socks off with what they could do.

When I showed anyone at Pratt my super realistic drawings of movie stars that had made most people drool before, they were now met with snickers and comments like, "What good is that?... A photograph can do that."

Unbeknownst to me, Norman Rockwell (my hero) was out, and abstract expression was in.

Part 2

Pratt Falls

In my first class, the teacher gave us some white paper and a black Conté Crayon. He then proceeded to instruct us to draw a yellow straw hat. I must have sat there for twenty minutes with my black Conté Crayon poised over the blank white paper. How in heaven's name is one supposed to draw a yellow straw hat with a black Conté Crayon on white paper?

"This is the beginning of the end," I thought. Everyone was busy drawing yellow hats, and my Conté Crayon was frozen to my fingers.

Maybe my mom was right. Taking a few teaching courses to fall back on might not be a bad idea.

"Now draw a red and green polka-dotted bow tie," he shouted out. Mr. Duncalf was what they called a foundation teacher.

The first year at Pratt was spent trying to discover what field of art you were best suited for. For the first few months at Pratt, I truly thought that I had been fooling myself all these years in thinking I was an artist. For the first time in my life, insecurity was rearing its ugly head.

Up until this juncture, I was Mr. Talented, the envy of all who claimed not to be able to draw a straight line. Of course, I never told any of those people that drawing a straight line was one of the most difficult things to do anyway.

For the first year at Pratt, I commuted, lugging art projects back and forth from Jersey to Brooklyn on buses and subways. It was interesting, to say the least.

I'll never forget having to build this architectonic problem made out of hundreds of Balsa Wood strips that took 10 or so hours to design and put together. Then there was the problem of how I was going to get it to Brooklyn intact.

On the bus, everyone looked as though they wanted to smash my delicate sculpture. I ended up staring down at least ten people.

Luckily the "A" train was reasonably empty that morning as was the "D" train. The platform at the DeKalb station had only a few people wandering around, and I sighed with relief having made it there safely, when suddenly out of nowhere this rotund woman came wobbling toward me at about one mile an hour. I stood there like a deer caught in the bright headlights of an oncoming car. She had all the room in the world to pass by me even if she had been the size of a Mack Truck, which by the way, isn't that much of an exaggeration, and whamo… She walked right into my sculpture, dashing it to the ground. What was even more exasperating, she kept on walking without saying a word. I was so stunned I couldn't even react. I just stood there holding the base to my sculpture as little pieces broke off in slow motion to the ground.

I brought the base to Mr. Duncalf, and all he could say was, "Nice base, where is the sculpture?"

This is the same sensitive guy who asked us to make colorful lyrical drawings with black Conté Crayons, who now looked upon my crushed design with not one speck of compassion. He was a strange cat if you don't mind my saying so. No matter what he was wearing, he always wore red socks. Now, what in the Sam Hill was that all about?

I remember taking this class on color with Miss Hertzler. We had to put together these Munsell Color Charts that had every shade and color imaginable. We were then asked to create a design utilizing these specific colors from the huge chart.

Lance Wyman, one of my best friends who just happened to grow up in the same town in New Jersey like me, thought it would be brilliant if we were to create an entire set of colors in little glass tubes that matched the colors on the chart. This way, all we would have to do is look up a number on the chart that corresponded to the number on the tube, and we would be way ahead of the game. It took us a solid week to prepare these tubes. Unfortunately, the project lasted about four weeks, and the paint dried out in three days.

That first year Lance and I commuted together with tackle boxes, books, pads, and three-dimensional designs in tow. On one crowded trip, Lance tried to make his way to the back of the bus with his heavy drawing pads over his head. Suddenly, the bus lurched forward, sending Lance running and tripping to the back like a human horizontal guillotine, finally smashing the stiff pads into the back window just above this woman's head. A little lower and she would have gone the way of Marie Antoinette.

On another memorable trip, we were sitting on the long last seat with our feet pressed together and our backs up against the rear side windows. We thought it would be funny to see who could push the hardest when all of a sudden, the window behind me flew out of the bus like a ballistic missile. We never did see where it landed as we sheepishly slid into the seat in front of us.

Lance was the only one that appreciated my realistic drawings of movie stars. In fact, I remember him saying that my drawings alone were enough to intimidate him, not to mention the fear and trepidation that came over him by seeing what art high school kids could do.

Not long after, however, our fears and trepidations became a thing of the past, and we began to be judged by what we were doing in the present, and not the baggage that we came there with.

That first year went by rather quickly, and Lance decided that his talents were best suited for the Industrial Design Department. I, of course, knew all along that

Advertising Design was for me, just like my cousin Vince DiGiacomo.

I felt like a grown-up in my second year as I focused in on the world of advertising design.

We had a lettering class taught by the famous abstract expressionist James Brooks who had been a lettering man in another incarnation. He approached the letterform from the negative shapes as well as the positive ones. We worked with everything from fine quill pens to Chinese calligraphy brushes.

One of my favorite projects was writing a word on white paper with rubber cement. When the rubber cement dried, we covered the rest of the page with black paint. When that dried, the rubber cement was removed, leaving a wonderful negative image.

We had drawing classes with another famous abstract expressionist, Jack Tworkov. He had us drawing the human body for over an hour with a very hard sharpened 4H pencil, holding it by the very end. In this particular exercise, the pencil never left the paper. It required concentration on a level that I had never experienced before.

Then he made us draw the same figure with a two-inch-wide paintbrush using black ink, and it had to be finished in 60 seconds. The contrast between the two techniques transformed my ability to see.

How exciting is that? I distinctly remember this

wonderful sense of freedom that came over me while experiencing doing what I loved so much.

No isosceles triangles or polygons here to deal with. No need to find out how many electrons there are in a hydrogen atom.

No, this is freedom of expression on an entirely new level, and to think it all started with drawing a picture of Mickey Mouse.

Herschel Levit: the Most Important Influence in My Life

Everyone at one time or another is exposed to a teacher who truly makes a difference in their life. In my case, it was a man by the name of Herschel Levit.

He was a talented, dramatic intellectual who inspired us with music, photography, and art. He was a great believer that anyone who was to become a great communicator and designer needed to fill oneself with all kinds of information. In order to draw on your interior computer bank, you had to fill it with information.

Sometimes he would bring in recordings of Enrico Caruso, the music of Leonard Bernstein, or slides of the architecture of Rome. Some of the students were actually upset with his idea of teaching, claiming that it was a design class, not a culture appreciation course.

They didn't understand and actually drew up a petition to have him removed. Santo Cambarrari, Marshall Arisman, and I knew that would be a huge mistake and made our way to the Dean's office to stand up for him.

Herschel was responsible for influencing hundreds of successful designers, art directors, photographers, and film directors like Sheila Metzner, Bob Giraldi, George Lois, and Stephen Frankfurt, who owe a great deal to him.

A Taste of Mad Ave

Every year one student was picked from the junior class to work for a very large advertising agency by the name of Young & Rubicam during the summer break. I was lucky enough to be the one chosen that year. How exciting is that?

I asked my mom if I could go to Brooks Brothers to buy the appropriate clothes. Madison Avenue was festooned with men in Grey Flannel suits, and I just had to have one. I bought a buttoned-down white shirt, and of course, a light blue one as well. Then I proceeded to the tie rack. Striped and paisley ties were the thing. Oh, and you had to have a pair of wing-tipped shoes and black knee socks to finish the image.

The year was 1959, and although Young & Rubicam was the largest Advertising Agency in the world at the time, air conditioning had not made its way to 285 Madison Avenue.

Instead, each room had a small motorized fan tucked away in one of its corners on a little shelf. However, the mat room (a place where ads were mounted for presentation purposes and art supplies were kept) had no fan, no windows, and no air, and that was where I spent the hottest summer of my life.

By the end of the summer, my wing-tipped shoes could actually fly on their own.

I remember taking a lunch break at a small coffee shop in the same building, hoping to find some relief from the heat. Unfortunately, being in the same building meant that they didn't have air-conditioning either.

This place was so small that their supply room was in the cellar, and as I walked in, I saw this black man rising from the floor behind the counter on a four-foot-square platform. He said as he wiped his brow, "Oi, Madone."

I thought, how interesting this multicultural city of ours is. Hot, but interesting.

I wanted so much to impress people and let everyone know that my cousin was the famous Vince DiGiacomo, the creator of the award-winning Hathaway Shirt Patch campaign.

How many know that the more you try to impress someone, the less impressive it is. Somehow the universe has a way of straightening you out.

Humble Class #101

One day I was in one of the stalls in the bathroom, and I could hear the creative director speaking to the head art director while using the urinals. In the process of replacing a roll of toilet paper, it dropped and rolled out and under the door close to the feet of the two chiefs. As I tried to reel it back in by gently pulling on the portion still in my hand, it continued to roll out even farther with each gentle tug. Finally, it ended up between the creative director's legs. He was kind enough to hand it back to me over the door, and I said in the deepest best-disguised voice I could, "Thank you."

Actually, it was one of the most productive summers of my life. I got to see some of the best artwork go through my mat room, and I had a chance to handle it up close. You could hardly pay for an education like that, and here I was being paid to do this.

Every day I had the opportunity to handle wonderful artwork by people like Norman Rockwell, Andy Warhol, Phil Hayes, Tom Allen, Tomi Ungerer, John Gundelfinger, Peter Max, Seymour Chwast, Daniel Schwartz, James McMullen, David Levine, Bernie Fuchs, Burton Silverman, Gerry Gersten, Milton Glaser, and Robert Weaver—just to name sixteen.

I shared this supply room, or mat room as it was called, with a man by the name of Dick Calderhead.

He was a recent graduate of the Yale School of Design. He was very bright, a bit older than me, and he seemed to approach advertising from a more intellectual point of view than from us Pratt guys. He taught me how to paint with watercolor paints, spit, and a little soap. Heavy, huh?

It was our responsibility to cut mats, frame advertising proposals that were to be presented at meetings with clients, and keep the supplies up to date.

I remember carrying a bunch of neatly matted double-page spread comprehensive layouts to the 10th floor boardroom. After turning them over to the creative team for presentation, I kind of hid in one corner of the room to get a first-hand look at how this impressive-looking meeting was to take place. Ten or so serious-looking people were surrounding the table, puffing on pipes, each one with a cup of coffee, a pad, and a perfectly sharpened yellow pencil with the Y&R logo on it.

I remember thinking, "This is what big business looks like." Then one of the silver-haired executives placed one of the Birds Eye double-page spreads in front of the client. The art director had rendered Birds Eye Frozen packages amongst a still life of vegetables. There was a long pause as the client perused the layout. The account executive took a puff on his pipe, and a long discussion ensued as they tried to determine if there were too many peas on the page.

I backed up against the wall and said to myself with confidence, "I can do this" and left the room.

It was a crazy summer. I remember making a trail of rubber cement with some other guys down the entire 8th-floor hall on the south side of the building into the room and under the desk of this old and totally unfriendly art director who used to fart a lot.

As if the farting wasn't bad enough, he was always excusing himself, so there was no way of making believe you didn't hear it.

Well anyway, we set this trail of rubber cement on fire and ran like the dickens to the opposite end of the floor. You could hear the trail of fire charging down the hall to his office. It was climaxed with a loud yelp, followed by some explicit commentary, then followed by him grabbing his coat and hat and leaving for the day!

He never mentioned that such a thing ever happened, and much to our amazement, we never heard him fart again either. We must have scared the crap out of him, so to speak!

Back to School

It was sad to see the summer end. Going back to Pratt after working the whole summer in the largest advertising agency in the world was really tough. Once I tasted the fruits of the real world of advertising, it was hard to go back to the land of dreams and possibilities.

I must admit I went back with a bit of an attitude.

Comments like, "That's not really how they do it in the business," didn't win me a lot of favor with my old friends.

Speaking of old friends, I think the person I miss most from Pratt was a girl by the name of Jill Symington. We were really close buddies. Although we were never romantically involved, we used to walk around the halls holding hands.

We consoled each other about everything and anything that was troubling us, and at that age, there always seemed plenty to be consoled about!

She only went to Pratt for a couple of years, but while she was there, we were practically inseparable.

One day our class's work was being critiqued by a teacher named Bob Dolce, and I was in the back of the room watching everyone get shot down except me. The competitive me reacted in an irresponsible way, by raising my fist to the heavens…Yeah!

I think the competitive thing never sat well with Jill,

and she especially didn't like seeing it in me. She was the only one to see and hear me, thank God, but the disappointment in her eyes toward me is etched in my psyche even to this day.

I think she cared for me more than as a buddy. I may be wrong, but there was this look in her eye that I would catch once in a while.

We were at the hall sinks one day, where we used to wash out our paintbrushes, and she was facing the mirror. I was standing behind her, holding a drawing pad in such a way that my muscles were popping out. She looked up, catching my image over her shoulder in the reflection and did a sort of swooning thing. I looked at her and said, "What?"

She didn't answer. She just looked down and continued to wash out her brushes. Unfortunately, I've lost touch with her, but to this day I look for her face in crowds, especially at museums and art galleries.

Then there were these two graduates from Industrial Arts High School that I also became friendly with, Mark Yustein and Tom Parmagianni. Every Friday evening after a long hard week, we would go our separate ways—Mark back to Jackson Heights, Queens, Tom to Bay Ridge, Brooklyn, and me to Kearny, New Jersey.

On Monday, the first thing we would do is get together in the Pie Shop for a weekend date report!

Between our junior and senior year, just before we

all separated for the summer, Tom thought he should clear something up with Mark and me.

He said, "You know when we come back every Monday and talk about our dating experiences?"

I said, "Yeah."

"Well, I was always talking about…guys!"

I was so naive then that I didn't even have a clue what he was trying to tell me. "You mean you double date with other guys?" I said.

"No, I date guys… I am gay."

There was a long pause while my brain frantically tried to assimilate that information.

"What does that mean?"

"I thought you both should know."

Suddenly all kinds of memories and flashbacks were going through my head all at once. We used to have swimming classes together, and don't ask me why, but in those days, the men all swam naked, something about the lint from the bathing suits clogging the filters. A flashback of Tom always walking behind me in those classes suddenly popped into my head and made me feel very uncomfortable.

The memory of his father working for the Capezio Shoe Company, which made all these feminine looking shoes for the New York Ballet, came rushing in also.

Tom delighted in giving me shoes every now and then. We must have looked like a couple walking the halls of Pratt together in those sweet-looking things.

How could I not have known? Three years hanging out with this guy, and I never even suspected for one second? You've got to be kidding me!

Somehow Mark and I got over the shock and tried to make believe that it really didn't matter. But I must admit, I was never ever comfortable in those swim classes after that!

In my senior year, I decided (with my parents' reluctant support) to get an apartment. I found this wonderful place across from Washington Park in an old brownstone. Unfortunately, it was on the fourth floor, and the walk-up carrying equipment was a bit of a buster!

My old friend from Kearny, Lance Wyman, roomed with me. I am sure Neil Simon observed us somehow because we were the original "Odd Couple."

We had a two-room apartment. We shared the large room, which included a kitchen of sorts. The second room was more like a closet than a room, and I used it for my drawing table and art equipment.

Unlike myself, Lance was working on a limited budget. He would make this huge pot of beef stew on Sunday night, and that would be his supper for the rest of the week. Actually, that wasn't a bad idea in that the stew included all the essential ingredients for a balanced diet, and it tasted pretty good too.

I always gave him a lot of credit for his determination

in fending for himself. In the summers, he would work in this incredibly hot bakery making bread. During the school season, he held down more than one job to pay for all his expenses.

Often on Sunday nights, I would come back with a care package that almost always included meatballs, sausage, and of course, our famous gravy. Lance always appreciated the change of pace.

Unfortunately, when I returned on Sunday night, I was greeted with a kitchen of stacked up pots, pans, dishes, and a few cockroaches.

My side of the room always looked neat and perfect, and his side of the room looked as though it had been caught up in some huge Cuisinart.

Me being the spoiled brat that I was, I never let him forget it, and it was a cause for some unpleasant moments, one that ended up with me throwing a metal stool at him. Fortunately, my aim was as bad as my temper.

Lance, having chosen Industrial Design as his major, didn't help matters much either. He was forever building something, so there was this ever-present cloud of sawdust and plaster powder from sanding hanging in the air. You'd wake up in the morning and swear that snow had fallen in the room.

I don't want to make it sound too horrible. We had a lot of fun that year also. We liked pulling pranks on each other, like filling the toothpaste tube with Brylcreem or refilling a cologne bottle with a nasty-smelling sulfur concoction.

Then there was the time I lifted the seat on the toilet, stretched plastic wrap over the bowl, and then set the lid back down again. You couldn't see that it was there for anything. Luckily for Lance, he had to tinkle first!

One night we had this shaving cream fight, which I might add wasn't confined to our room. We carried it all the way out into the hallway, spraying each other right up to the front door of the neighbors in the next apartment. Although the couple living there were good friends and classmates of ours, they weren't too happy with our childish shaving cream war! They were recently married, and I believe Lance and I were infringing on their romantic first year together.

One afternoon after classes were over, I decided to buy a pizza and bring it back to the apartment. I was carrying one of those large art pads, so I put the pizza under my arm supported by the drawing pad and proceeded to walk home. When I opened the pizza box, there was no topping on it. It was pure dough. I looked down at my shoe, which was covered with tomato sauce and mozzarella. I then noticed that there was this neat trail from my foot to the closed door. I opened it, walked over to the stairwell, and peeked over the railing to find a perfect pizza trail up the entire four flights.

Upon graduation, which I don't mind saying that I made the Dean's List, I was lucky enough to be the first person from the summer program at Young & Rubicam to be hired back.

My mother never actually said how proud she was of me. But I was blown away when she handed me the keys to a brand new 1960 beige Chevy Impala with a rust-colored interior.

Part 3

Y&R Here I Come…

Right back where I started from.

Right back, right back into the mat room, I might add. This time I got to share the mat room with this 18-year-old string bean phenom by the name of Jeff Metzner. He didn't even go to college, but boy was he talented!

He wore his black pants so tight his legs looked like licorice sticks. Actually, you never knew what he was going to look like from one day to the next. One day he would come in with the frizzies, and the next day he would shave his head. His personality was as big as his talent, and quite frankly, I was a little intimidated by him.

I was much more conservative than Jeff. And when you're trying to work your way up in a company like Young & Rubicam, you have to make yourself known somehow.

Jeff was promoted out of the mat room as an assistant art director to the only other Italian in the company beside the shoeshine guy and me. His name was Tony Carillo, probably the nicest person I ever met.

Tony started at Y&R at 16 years old, and at age 36, he already had 20 years in the company profit-sharing program. We were always trying to figure out how much Tony must be worth because he was forever walking around with this incredible smile on his face.

Years later, Tony's daughter, Mary Carillo, became a celebrity tennis player and then a TV announcer.

Y&R boasted quite a few famous people, mostly in the arts, however. Bob Cottingham became one of the most celebrated photo-realistic painters in the world. Rowland B. Wilson was one of the best-known cartoonists *Esquire* magazine ever employed. And Stephen Frankfurt, who came up through the new medium called television, not only wound up as president of Y&R, he also created the 1962 award-winning credits for the movie *To Kill a Mockingbird.*

It was a blessing to be surrounded by so much talent. In those days, if you couldn't draw, you were in trouble. There was no such thing as a computer, no Internet to check for stock photos, and the only Google was in the song, *Barney Google (with the Goo-Goo-Googly Eyes).* The art directors at Y&R were great artists. Years before I got into the business, comprehensive layouts were done in pastel. And at Y&R, there were still a few of those guys around. Most of the guys, however, were doing their layouts in watercolor or Magic Markers.

Thankfully I liked to draw, and I learned a ton from people like Rowland B. Wilson, who utilized the same exact technique for his famous cartoons as he used for making his layouts.

I guess I was fairly good at it because not long after Jeff Metzner became an assistant, I was picked to be an assistant to one of the supervisors by the name of Mason Clark.

Mason was responsible for the General Foods account, and I loved doing comprehensive layouts on all kinds of foods like Birds Eye Frozen Food, Instant Sanka, Brim, Jell-O, and Gaines-Burgers Dog Food. I even worked on Chef Boyardee Ravioli, but I never let my Sicilian mother know about that one.

Now that I was an assistant art director, I was in the position to order artwork, photography, and retouching. And not long after, I was asked to go to lunch with this photographer's representative. Naturally, he spent most of the time touting his photographer, and at one point promised to pay me a fee each time I was to use him. I was so naive at the time I just thought that this was so wonderful of him. "I mean, I can use any photographer I want… but if I use this guy, I can supplement my income, wow!" I said to myself.

When I went back to the office, I was so excited that I went right into Mason Clark's office and told him of the good news. Halfway through my first sentence, Mason put his pointer finger to his mouth, closed the door, and said, "Shh… You can't do that. That's payola!"

"What's payola?" I said innocently.

Well, Mason read me the full and complete riot act and opened my eyes to a world that I could not have even imagined existed. Existed … why there was a man at the agency that turned payola into an art form!

This guy's responsibility was as Head Art Buyer. In other words, when you wanted to purchase any form of art, you had to go through him. He would write out the purchase orders and so on.

He fancied himself an artist himself and actually exhibited his own watercolors on a rotating basis on the walls of his office. I say rotating because art reps would come into his office and purchase his watercolors…all the time! Cute… Huh?

The advertising business in those days was a pretty WASPy (White Anglo Saxon Protestant) place to be, and if you had dark hair and a nose, you were definitely looked at with some trepidation.

But with people like George Lois and Bill Bernbach breaking the creative sound barrier, things were changing, and they were changing fast.

As I said, there were three Italians at Y&R in 1960, Tony Carillo, the shoeshine guy, and myself! There were a few Jewish copywriters, one Jewish art director, and one Jewish supervisor. The creative revolution that was exploding was mostly promulgated by ethnics. The art directors were either Italian or Greek, and the writers were predominately Jewish, with a few Irishmen thrown in.

One day the WASPy head art director and the WASPy creative director got the bright idea of creating a print ad campaign for Four Roses using real people to keep up with what was going on with the new creative explosion.

They approached the Jewish supervisor, I believe his name was Art Harris, and Tony Carillo, the Italian Art Director, to create a real-people campaign, which meant no blonds with freckles… I think.

Actually, that was an exciting moment and a great opportunity to do a breakthrough campaign.

Well, charged with that assignment, the ethnic creative team sought to employ an ethnic photographer by the name of Howard Zieff. Howard was famous for shooting realistic ethnic type photographs of people with actual color tones in their skin and even dark hair.

Obviously, Howard looked to his friends for subjects rather than the model agencies, which were mostly known for their six-foot blonds with blue eyes. Howard produced some extraordinary photos of people in drinking situations as never seen before in advertising. He was a genius.

Excited by the results, Tony Carillo (the Italian Art Director) walked down the hallway, photos in hand, and presented the pictures to Art Harris (the Jewish Supervisor). In turn, Art (the Jewish Supervisor), equally excited by the photographs, proceeded to go into a closed-door meeting with the two WASPy department heads.

Waiting to hear the result was not unlike waiting

for your first child to be born.

The reaction from the WASPy boys was mind-blowing, to say the least. "Why these photographs are very natural, but the models look too...too... Italian!"

The Jewish Supervisor brought the photos back to Tony Carillo (the Italian Art Director). "So...what did they think?" Tony asked excitedly.

There was a long and uncomfortable pause, and Art (the Jewish supervisor) finally spit it out, "They said the people look too Italian."

With smoke billowing out of his ears, Tony burst into the WASPy department head's office, jeopardizing his 20 years of profit sharing. "What do you mean these people look too Italian?"

Another long and awkward pause followed, and the WASPy creative director finally muttered, "I never said that ... what I said was ... they look too Jewish!"

Somehow these suits never got it. To this day, I don't know what they considered real people to look like.

Their answer to everything was always, "Sure, that concept will fly here in New York and California, but what about middle America? They'll never buy into this kind of forward-thinking."

Someone, somehow, had convinced them all that middle America was filled with uneducated, unsophisticated, and downright stupid people.

One exciting thing did happen not long after the

Four Roses fiasco, however. There was a company-wide gang-bang pitch called for on the Life Savers account, which meant anyone and everyone was allowed to present their ideas for a new set of full-page ads that would eventually appear in *Life* magazine. This was exciting. These were going to be full-color ads that would be seen by millions of people.

I created a bunch of them, but the one I liked best was so simple that I knew right from the get-go that it had real possibilities of making it.

I took the five different flavored Life Savers candies and laid them down on a white piece of paper as though I was doing an addition problem. I included the + sign and drew a line beneath the five zeros. I then added the numeral 5 with a headline that read, "Life Savers, they add up to 5 delicious flavors."

I submitted my ideas and one day later received a call for a six-month tour of active duty to Fort Dix in South Jersey with the National Guard.

I turned the keys to my Chevy Impala over to my girlfriend, Fran Bongiovanni, and off I went.

NG22012011

They gave us these dog tags to wear around our necks with our serial numbers on them. The first question I asked was, "Why are there these little grooves on either end of the dog tags … Sir!"

"Those are there so that when you get your dumb ass shot off, someone can wedge the tags between your teeth, and they'll know who and where to ship your sorry ass," said Platoon Sergeant Richard Lambert of Company "O" Third Training Regiment.

He had the face, body, and voice of an overgrown rat. His teeth would begin to protrude out of his mouth a split second before his high-pitched voice would start screaming like a banshee.

He started screaming at us from the moment we got off the bus on October 2nd, 1960, until the day we got shipped out eight weeks later to Fort Jackson, South Carolina for our infantry training.

The first few days of Basic Training were about standing in long lines. Long lines to get your hair shaved off. Long lines to get your clothes.

"Excuse me, Sir but these clothes are much too small for me. I weigh around 230 pounds, and they'll never fit," I said.

"By the time you finish Basic Training, they will fit you like a glove … now shut up and move along," screamed the Supply Sergeant.

This skinny little guy next to me held up his clothes and said, "Sir, these clothes are way too big for me ... Sir."

"By the time you finish Basic Training, they will fit you like a glove. Now, shut up and move along!" screamed the Supply Sergeant. I guess Sergeants must have to take a course in screaming to get those stripes on their arms; they're all so good at it.

Then there were the long lines for medical examinations. The first room is where you take everything off, and while holding your clothes, you go from one room to the next having different parts of your body probed. I've got to believe that this part was perhaps even tougher for the doctors than it was for us.

"Spread your legs, soldier," the doctor said. You see, he was a First Lieutenant, and they didn't scream for some reason.

With that, he thrust his two fingers under my testicles and asked me to cough. I turned my head to the right and coughed!

He smiled at me and said, "You're a college graduate, right?"

I said, "Yes, Sir... How did you know that, Sir?"

"You're the first person in the last fifty men that had the decency to turn your head when you coughed."

From there we went into this room where we were all handed little plastic bottles and asked to pee in them.

Now I have to tell you, it is no easy task to pee in a little plastic bottle while holding onto your entire wardrobe—boots and all. Guys were overflowing their bottles all over the place, and there was no way that I was going to put my clothes down anywhere.

The blood test was the most fun for me. They placed us in chairs all around the perimeter of the room, so that at one point, we were all facing each other. As the doctor found the vein in one of the soldier's arms and began to extract a vial of blood, the man directly across the room fainted. This caused a domino effect, and guys began falling like bowling pins all over the room... Bam! Right on their faces!

In the next room, I got another "You're a college graduate, aren't you?" comment. This time because I was the first person in the last fifty men who had all his teeth. I think that the fifty guys that were ahead of me were making me look really good!

One of the first warnings that circulates in Basic Training is to never volunteer for anything. But when old rat face Lambert asked if there was an artist in the group, I was so excited to be able to claim that distinction I forgot myself and raised my hand and yelled out loud, "Yes sir ... I am an artist!"

Lambert shot back, "Good, 'cause we have about fifty butt-cans that need to be repainted."

Butt-cans are old coffee cans half-filled with water

that get nailed to the posts on the support beams in the barracks for smelly cigarette butts. It was now my job not only to paint each one of them the color red but also to keep them emptied and cleaned for the next eight weeks.

I've got to tell you, Basic Training was no picnic. We even had a couple of deaths during our eight weeks at Fort Dix.

In learning how to throw a hand grenade, one needs to engage the grenade by pulling the pin with your left hand while holding down the pressured lever with the thumb of your right hand. You draw the grenade back next to your right ear while extending your left hand toward the desired target. You then drop the pin, release the pressure lever, count to three, and throw the grenade as far as you can.

Somehow this left-handed kid got all mixed up and threw the pin and held the grenade, blowing his head off, as well as killing the sergeant who was in the foxhole with him.

This happened a few days before my platoon was up for the same drill. Based on the experience of the left-handed kid with no head, I decided to keep letting the Gung Ho Guys go ahead of me in line. I never did end up throwing one of those things.

Then there was the long crawl under barbed wire … in the mud, while cradling your M1 … with bullets flying overhead not more than ten inches above our heads.

My friend didn't believe that they would endanger us like that with live ammunition. "They're shooting blanks; who are they kidding?" he said. With that, he loosened the strap on his helmet and threw it up in the air. It came crashing and smoking to the ground with at least three bullet holes in it. Not only did he pee in his pants out of fear, but he ended up having to pay for the damn thing.

I remember this kid, Anthony Integlia. He just wasn't cut out for any of this army crap, and I truly felt for him. None of us were actually thrilled to be there, but Anthony was literally shaking in his boots the entire time.

We had another crawling episode under barbed wire, and somewhere in the middle of the crawling, they doused us with a heavy-duty exposure of tear gas. We were instructed to calmly remove our helmets, calmly put on our gas masks, calmly clear the mask by blowing through the mouthpiece, calmly put our helmets back on, and calmly proceed to crawl our way out of the area.

Unfortunately, Anthony, in clearing his mask must have sucked in air instead of blowing it out and inhaled a mouthful of tear gas. With tear gas burning his eyes and throat, poor Anthony panicked and stood up in the middle of the barbed wire. It ripped up his clothes as well as his skin, and to make matters worse, they made him go through it again.

On another occasion, to experience the latest military might of the United States Army, we were given the wonderful opportunity of shooting shoulder bazookas.

It's a two-man operation. One man in a kneeling position holds the weapon on his shoulder and aims it at the target ready to fire, while the second man loads the ammunition from the rear. The loader then attaches a little electrical wire connection, taps the shooter on top of the helmet signaling that the weapon is ready to be fired. He then ducks away careful not to go anywhere near the back of the bazooka because the backblast could easily take your face off.

I was the loader for this spastic-pear-shaped guy by the name of Peter M. Siegal, who must be related to the left-handed headless guy because as soon as I attached the wire, without waiting for the tap on the helmet, he shot the thing off which caused me to literally do a complete backflip … from a squatting position mind you.

As I said before, when I arrived at Fort Dix, I was overweight. I looked like a 230-pound Italian sausage that had turned moldy in my olive-green fatigues.

Every morning the bugler blasted us out of our beds at reveille. We collected ourselves around the trough to pee. You haven't lived until you've experienced the yellow river that early in the morning.

I love the smell of urine in the morning.

Making the bed tight enough to bounce a quarter off it came fairly easy to me, but the ten chin-ups before breakfast was something else.

Speaking about breakfast, I think I was the only person in the whole Rainbow Division that liked SOS (Shit On a Shingle). It was a kind of creamy chipped beef thing on toast. Go figure!

After breakfast, we made this five-mile forced march two by two out to the training fields. It took me two weeks to discover that you don't want to find yourself at the end of the formation. There is an accordion effect that happens which keeps the slow and chunky guys in the back running the entire five miles. I used to throw up my SOS at the same place on the road every morning.

I remember calling my dad one night, almost crying about how hard that five-mile forced march was. My dad paused for a second, then asked, "Are there telephone poles on the road?" I said there are, and then he said something brilliant... "You don't have to march the five miles. You just have to march from one telephone pole to the next. And eventually you will be there!" It worked, and before the eight weeks were up, I was marching out in front, carrying the flag and leading the company. He always had great little life-changing comments like that. I always found it fascinating how my father got smarter the older I got.

Well, the supply sergeant didn't lie. By the time Basic Training was over, I went from 230 lbs to 169 lbs, and my uniform fit like a glove. I lost over 60 lbs, and that skinny guy I told you about? He gained about 25 lbs. And guess what. His uniform fit like a glove.

Yankees in Redneck Country

For our Infantry Training, our entire unit was shipped out to Fort Jackson, South Carolina, to a language that none of us could understand.

"Yanks, y'all fall in nah. Picup em butts, Yanks. Wanna see asses ain elbas. Remember yer ass is grass an ahs da lawn mowwa!"

Lordy, Lordy, where in heaven's name am I?

"Yer lef ... Yer lef ... Yer lef, raht lef. Soun auf one two thiree foe ... soun auf. Ya had agood hom whnya lef. Ya had agood hom whnya lef ... Soun auf! Cadenz count, one two thiree foe.

Roll call in the morning was something to behold also. Most of us from the New York/New Jersey area were Jewish, Black, Greek, Italian, or Irish, and they made mincemeat out of each and every name!

"Private Ronald Traviannna?" "Here, Sir!"

"Private Peter M. Seegail!" "That's Siegel, Sir."

"That's what I said son, Seegail."

"Yes, Sir!"

"Well are you here or not, Private M. Seegail?"

"Here, Sir!"

"Private James C. Qu...eeee...bec."

"That's Quebec, Sir."

"I didn't ask whar ya from boy, I asked if ya war here."

"Here, Sir!"

The buildings looked the same. The uniforms looked the same. There was the same coal-burning smell out of the barracks mixed with the aroma of pine trees, but I've got to tell you, I felt as though I had been shipped off to some foreign country or something!

They put all the Yankees on the first floor of the barracks and all the Rebs on the second… Big mistake! The pushing and shoving started first thing in the morning at the yellow river trough.

"You I-talian, Yank?"

"You a Redneck, Reb?"

That night all hell broke loose. We all lost our weekend passes and ended up spit polishing the entire barracks. They ended up mixing us all together, which as it turned out, was a much better way to go.

I befriended the guy in the bunk above me who was in tremendous pain because he had never worn shoes before, and his feet were actually bleeding.

We had one black guy with us from New York by the name of Paul R. Miller, and he was cause for much discussion every night.

"I ain't sleepen under no n_ _ _ _ _," said one of the more friendly Rednecks.

Now you have to understand, we weren't used to hearing that kind of out-and-out prejudice back home, but these guys threw around that word like it was a term of endearment.

I actually started holding discussion groups at night trying to get to the bottom of where their prejudice lived.

"Listen, why do you hate Paul so much? You only met a few days ago, what could he have done in that time to…"

"He didn' do nuthin' ta me."

"Then why do you hate him so?"

"Cause he's a n_ _ _ _ _."

"Cut the crap. Why do you dislike him?"

"I don know jus do … tha's all! My pappy said they ain't worth spit."

Then one of the Rebs by the name of Robert T. Daugharty stepped forward.

"We don't all feel the same way this feller do. Pay you no mind to him. Hog's smarter than him. I'm from Valdosta, Georgia, glad ta meet ya, Yank."

I took a liking to this guy right away!

"You ever heard of Vidalia Onions? They're so good ya'll can eat 'em like you was eatin' apples."

On our first weekend leave Paul Miller, Bruce Todres, Robert T. Daugharty, Angelo Morringello (You can't believe how they massacred that name), and I went into Columbia for some real food.

"Don say I didn' warn ya… we's gonna have problems eatin' en a rest-o-rant with Paul. Mind ya, I don' have no problem with him, but yer in Columbia, South Carolina… This ain't New York City," said Robert T.

"Listen Robert T., (I always called him Robert T. or just plain Reb, he like dat!) I hear what you're saying, but we're in uniform. We represent the United States of America Armed Forces, for God's sake!" I blurted out with pride and confidence.

We sat down at a table in the first restaurant we came to, and before you could say cornbread and chitlins, the waitress came over to our table, pointing to Paul Miller.

"Y'all can't eat here… not with him anyways," she said.

I was blown away… I mean, I had heard of this outrageous Southern prejudice before, but I had never experienced it. We're talking 1960 now! This was five years after Rosa Parks took her seat in history at the front of the bus, and just a few years before the March on Washington.

"I warned ya… Ah tol' y'all, we was gonna have an issha," said Robert T.

Paul said, "Listen, you guys. Stay, I'll find something."

"No way, if you can't stay, none of us will," said Morringello. I mean, the water fountains were marked "Whites Only," and public toilets for blacks were always in the rear somewhere.

I never could, not for the life of me, understand how this kind of prejudice could exist in an area considered to be the Bible Belt.

Doesn't it say somewhere in the Bible that we are to love our fellow man as we do ourselves? I guess all these "good old boys" must not like themselves very much.

One evening I was running toward the mess hall when a familiar voice rang out, "Ron." I turned, and to my amazement, found Mark Yustein, my buddy from Pratt Institute, standing there.

"Wow, how much weight did you lose?" he shouted in disbelief. "About 60... you look like you put on a couple!"

"Yeah," he said, "My uniform finally fits like a glove."

Mark was one cycle ahead of me, which meant that he would be getting out eight weeks before me.

He and a group of other guys had somehow found a way to get themselves attached to S3 (the Operations & Training Office), where they were working on the Battalion Newspaper. One guy was actually teaching algebra to the Colonel. Go figure!

At the risk of sounding prejudiced myself, I have to tell you that the whole bunch of them were Jewish. They must be God's chosen people, or they're just plain smart. But there they were, finishing out their Army obligation in a warm office with cookies and fresh coffee every day, while the Goyim were out freezing their butts off on bivouac. Mazel tov!

Speaking about bivouac, not long after that connection with Mark, I was one of those Goyim out there freezing my butt off. The first night it rained, then snowed, and the tent froze into this wonderful glistening shelter that I was to call home for the next few days!

I shared the tent with this guy that I really didn't know, but what I remember about him the most was that he stuttered… a lot… and long!

"Mamamma na..na..naame is Ro..ro..rob..bb bert Ta..ta..ttt..ow ntat..ownsend Jr..jr..jrrrunior," he sa..sa.. sssaid.

I remember my mother telling me once in an effort to teach me how important it was to hang out with the right people, "If you walk long enough with a man that limps, you will eventually find yourself limping."

That message rang loud and clear one morning when I went to order my breakfast. "I'lll hha..hh..avae ss..ss..ooos..ss pa..pa..palease!"

Well, one night soon after, I woke up to the ice-coated tent completely collapsed and on my face. I tried to right it while still inside the tent, but I could see that wouldn't work. So, I climbed out of my sleeping bag (in my underwear and bare feet, I might add) and went outside to fix it.

We had a class specifically dealing with sleeping bags. It was their theory that you actually would keep warmer with fewer clothes on in a sleeping bag than you would with all your clothes on.

I don't know what genius came up with that concept,

but I remember wishing that he had been there to help me put up the tent! And I guess stuttering makes you sleep better cause 'ol Ta..ta..ta..own..ssss..end slept through the whole thing!

The following night a jeep pulled up to our campsite, and an MP delivered what must have been important information for our Staff Sergeant. It was actually orders to have me brought back to the company area. I was frightened to death. Thoughts raced through my mind… Could one of my parents have died? What could I have done that would have an MP drive all the way out here with special orders to get me?

"Grab all you gear together Travianna, you're going back to the company headquarters," shouted the Staff Sergeant.

That ride back to the Company was one of the loneliest and scariest moments of my life. I couldn't imagine what could have happened. I was pretty sure that I had done nothing wrong, so it must be that someone in my family must have died.

I reported to my Company Commander, who was the only person left behind in the Company. I snapped to attention and shouted out, "Private Travisano reporting as ordered, Sir!"

"At ease, soldier. I got an order from S3 that you are to report there tomorrow morning at 0700. Get a haircut, spit-shine your boots, and don't even think about being late. Do you hear me, private?"

"Yes, Sir! May I ask a question, Sir?"

"Yes."

"Why do they want to see me? Did I do something wrong, Sir?"

"I actually don't know, soldier, but it must be important for them to haul you all the way back from bivouac."

Well, that conversation did little to assuage my fears. I got my haircut, spit-polished my shoes, shined my brass, got my dress greens pressed, and took the coldest shower I ever had in my life.

Since the company was out on bivouac, the heat was turned off in the barracks, which meant that there wasn't any hot water either. I actually had to scream through the process of washing off the soap from my body!

The next morning, I put on my dress greens and reported to S3 promptly at 0700 hours. As the doors swung open, I once again snapped to attention, screaming out, "Private Travisano reporting as ordered, Sir!"

I was met with a cacophony of belly laughs as the doors parted. Guys were rolling on the floor with laughter. It was my friend Mark Yustein and his buddies who had sent a letter to my company commander, written by them on S3 letterhead, ordering me to report there ASAP.

I couldn't believe it. These nuts could have been court-martialed!

They introduced me to the editor of the Battalion Newspaper, Sergeant Alan Schuster.

"I hear you're an assistant art director for Young & Rubicam Advertising Agency in New York," he said.

"Yes, Sir."

"How would you like to report here every day to work on the Battalion Newspaper?"

I looked around the room at the crazy people that got me here. They were all smiling like Cheshire Cats.

"Yes Sir, I would like that very much."

"Great. I'll send an order to your company commander that you are to report here at 0700 hours every day from here on out. By the way, do you know how to shag golf balls?"

My main responsibility was to go to the library every day and copy an article from a book that had hundreds of accounts of soldiers who had been awarded the Purple Heart. My second responsibility was to shag some golf balls for the Sergeant.

I walked back and forth from the library to S3 every day from then on with a clipboard in one hand, and you would be amazed at how many people saluted me. In fact, it is amazing what you can get away with in the Army by just walking around with a clipboard.

One day while flipping through the Purple Heart Book in the library for our next story, I noticed the librarian place a new issue of *Life* magazine on the table.

I could have sworn I saw my Life Savers ad on the back cover as she put it down.

I immediately ran to the table and much to my delight, it was my ad. I couldn't believe it, my ad, on the back page of *Life* magazine. I showed it to the librarian and told her that I had created it.

"That's nice," she said. I don't think she believed a word of it. She must have a hundred soldiers hitting on her every day, telling her one line or another to impress her.

Somehow we got Robert T. Daugharty to work on the Battalion Newspaper to help give us that Southern touch. He and I became such good friends that to this day, we still talk on the phone, and he is forever sending me Vidalia onions, or some ol' homemade salad dressing, or *sumtin'*.

Well, my tour of duty was coming to a close, and I could hardly wait to get home to the love of my life. I was also anxious to see if she had done any damage to my new Chevy Impala.

I could barely get to sleep those last nights. I was constantly fantasizing how I would throw my duffel bag over my shoulder, run up the steps to her house two at a time, enter the front door, slip into her room while placing my duffel bag on the floor, and walk over to the side of her bed. All in slow motion of course. The moonlight would be shining through the blinds, her hair flowing over her pillow. Then I would lean over and gently kiss her on the lips.

Finally, the time came. We were released a day or two earlier than had been expected, so I thought I would play out my fantasy to the hilt.

Just before I got on the plane to fly home, I called her and told her I wouldn't be home for a couple of days. I arrived at her house late that same night by taxi. I threw my duffel bag over my shoulder, took the stairs two at a time to her front door, went into the house, then quietly slipped into her room, and there she was. The moonlight was falling across her face and pillow. Her hair was glistening, and her lips were moist. Everything was exactly how I had pictured it. I gently leaned over to kiss her, and she jumped up out of bed—screaming!

Her parents came running into the room. God only knows what they thought I had done to her.

Y&R—Back Again

The first person I saw when I came back was a guy by the name of Larry Leblanc. He actually didn't recognize me.

"May I help you?" he asked as I stood in the doorway to his office.

"Larry, it's me, Ron… I'm back."

"Oh, wow… How much weight did you lose? You look like a nose with two legs."

Larry always had a charming way with words.

We had a terrific bunch of young assistant art directors at Y&R, and almost every one of them went on to do very well in the business.

I was pulling down a huge salary of $75.00 a week, and embarrassingly enough, my girlfriend Fran was making $125.00.

We were getting pretty serious, and not long after my return from the olive drab world of the Armed Forces, I decided to ask her to marry me.

I went and bought a ring and decided that it would be incredibly romantic to drive up to West Orange, where there was a park with a spectacular view of New York City's glistening lights. Unfortunately, I was a mess from the moment we left the house until we got there and as Mortimer Snerd, Charlie McCarthy's sidekick once said, "My tongue got in the way of my eye tooth, and I couldn't see what I was saying."

To make matters even worse, when I opened the handkerchief that held the engagement ring, it fell to the ground. I quickly and gracefully rescued it from the mud and placed it on her finger.

"Wi…wi…ll.. y.. y.. y.. you ma… marry… mmm… me?" I said with all the control and verbal skills of Porky Pig.

I knew I wanted to marry her before I even met her. I remember pointing her out to my sister at Church one day, "You see that girl? I am going to marry her someday."

I may be a klutz, but you have to admit, I'm a prophetic klutz!

We were married on June 10, 1961. I spent the day before our wedding being operated on in the hospital for a staphylococcus infection in the palm of my hand. I must have contracted it somehow in the army hospital where I had been quarantined with mumps just before coming home.

I was released from the hospital the morning of our wedding, and when the packing was removed from my hand, it would not stop bleeding. We were continuously wrapping and rewrapping my hand right up to the moment of her walking down the aisle.

When we knelt at the altar, I looked up at a statue of Jesus and focused for some reason on the nail wounds in the palms of His hands. Call it what you will, but all I can tell you is the bleeding stopped right then and there.

We spent our wedding night at a hotel near Idlewild Airport, now known as John F. Kennedy International Airport. The first thing we ordered to our room was a pot of boiling water to wash out the wound in my hand. The hotel people, knowing we were honeymooners, must have been scratching their heads, trying to figure out why a newly married couple needed boiling water so soon after they were married.

The next morning we left for San Juan, Puerto Rico. Up until then, my only exposure to anything Puerto Rican was the Broadway show *West Side Story*. I must tell you Leonard Bernstein's music captured the essence and liveliness of the people of this Island Paradise!

El Morro Castle, aqua-colored water, incredible food, music, and dancing in the streets (everywhere!) made for a wonderful start to our honeymoon.

Then we were off to Haiti.

Now I am not a prejudiced person, but I felt uncomfortable from the moment we stepped off the plane. I had never been in a place where I was the minority, and to make matters even more uncomfortable, everywhere we went, everyone was staring at us. I mean, these were the kind of stares that could make your toes curl.

We were greeted at the plane by a government official named Obay. It was his job to make visiting tourists feel at home. As far as we were concerned, he had his work cut out for him.

We took an incredibly long ride through the countryside and finally up a huge mountain to our hotel, the whole time being stared at from people along the road. It was as though they had never seen a white person before.

The hotel was a tad shabby looking and wasn't exactly jumping with the excitement and color that we had experienced in Puerto Rico. When we were shown the room, there was black soot all over the white bedspread, and Fran began to cry uncontrollably.

We didn't even unpack. We took the same taxi back to the center of town to an empty but far more luxurious hotel. At least there wasn't any soot on the bed. We had heard that the Hotel Oloffson was wonderful, but if we weren't gay, we probably wouldn't feel comfortable there. So far, there wasn't much that we were comfortable with, including Obay.

We got so paranoid about being there that we went right to a travel agent and changed our plans to leave the very next day to Nassau in the Bahamas.

That night, however, Obay tried to warm us up by escorting us to what he called a traditional Voodoo ceremony. It was the tourist trap of tourist traps—where crazed people danced, screamed a lot, cut the head off a chicken, and then proceeded to drink its blood.

Good move, Obay! That did wonders to make us

feel good about being there.

Papa Doc was in power at the time, and it was clear that there were the haves and the have-nots, but I mean have naught, nothing, nada, como un zero, niente, nicht, and as they say in French, "moins que rien."

Strange as it may sound, by the time we were ready to leave the next day, we fell in love with the place and were sorry for having changed the reservations. The people that were staring at us were not threatening but interested. We visited the Barbancourt Rum Castle, bought hand made wooden salad bowls, ate frozen flavored ice cones, took pictures of some of the most beautiful smiling faces I have ever seen, shopped till we almost dropped, and made it to the plane with tears in our eyes just in time.

Nassau was as boring as it was beautiful, so we didn't stay there very long either and headed for the next mistake—Miami, Florida!

We stayed at one of those honeymoon hotels, where all the sunburned newlyweds get sloshed on drinks in coconut shells with funny little umbrellas sticking out of them. I think the hotel was called the Beachcomber or the Sunrise Clipper-joint-something.

At the pool, they had this guy from "Hawaii" weaving hats out of palm branches and a poor man's imitation of Don Ho singing the Hawaiian wedding song (*Ke Kali Nei Au*).

It kind of reminded me of when I was a kid playing on the street in front of my house. At least twice every summer, this Hawaiian dude with a flowered shirt would show up in a colorful truck with palm trees painted on it. He had this speaker on top of his truck playing a medley of songs by Haleloke, and that old favorite—*Mele Kalikimaka* with Arthur Godfrey singing along, accompanying her on his Ukulele!

The dude sold Yo-Yos, and for merely 25 cents extra, he would whip out his knife and carve your name on it.

Somehow in today's culture, I have a hard time picturing a grown man talking to kids on some suburban street selling Yo-Yos and wielding a knife. I just don't think that would cut it—excuse the pun.

Back to the honeymoon!

One morning we had breakfast on Collins Avenue amongst some of the oldest people on our planet. After watching them for one hour stealing all the Sweet'n Low sugar packets, and cellophane-wrapped saltines, we decided that perhaps it was time to cut our honeymoon short and go home to our new apartment at 202 Union Avenue in Rutherford, New Jersey.

Do you recall my mentioning that staphylococcus infection in my hand at the beginning of our honeymoon? Well, somehow, it ended up on Fran's stomach the minute we got home! Go figure!

And Then There Were Three

My wife began throwing up about two weeks after we got home, and I was praying that it had nothing to do with a lack of sexual prowess on my part. But alas, a glow came to her face, her period ceased, and she began sending me out to get her hot dogs at 11:30 at night. Nine months and two weeks later, our first son was born, which prompted all of our aunts to suddenly begin counting on their fingers.

Since my wife had been a secretary and I was an assistant art director, I thought it clever to design a birth announcement with a picture of one of those round erasers with a brush attachment next to an artist's paintbrush on the cover. Then when you turned the page, it revealed a smaller version of the artist's paintbrush and the announcement.

Vincent Philip Travisano was born on a Monday, April 2, 1962, weighing in at 8 pounds 11 ounces with ten fingers and ten toes. Alleluia!

I remember walking all the way up 38th Street from the Port Authority to Young & Rubicam at 285 Madison Avenue, saying out loud, "I have a son, a son... me... I have a son... I have a son! Wow!"

After passing out cigars to everyone in sight, I decided to call Vincent DiGiacomo, my famous art director cousin, to tell him that I had named my son after him. It took a while for him to come to the phone, and when he did, he sounded extremely weak. I could barely hear his voice.

"Vince, I just wanted you to know that my wife and I just had a baby boy and … and we named him Vincent … after you."

"That's wonderful, Ronnie. Listen to me now— don't ever let them get to you. They'll try to eat you up, but don't let them. Stand your ground, you hear?"

That sounded like a man speaking his last words, and when I hung up, I immediately called my mother to see what was going on with him.

Vince was born with a weak heart right from the get-go. He was never expected to live past 20. That was new information for me, and I must say, it kind of took the steam out of me.

By Friday, I received the bad news that he had passed away.

Incredible… Here I was, honoring the man who had inspired me to do what I was doing in the world by naming my firstborn after him, and then he dies the very same week.

Well, before he left us, he not only made his mark in the world of advertising, but he made an incredible mark on me that has guided me in my career to this very day.

I worked at Y&R for about two and a half years

before my friend, Jeff Metzner, told me he was offered an assistant art director job at McCann Marschalk.

Marschalk, as it was referred to, was a hot creative shop at the time, and a move like that could only benefit a young creative person on the way up.

Not long after Jeff was working there, he called to tell me that there was another job for an assistant opening and that I should get my book up there as quickly as possible.

I met with this Senior Associate Creative Director by the name of Hank Seiden. There was no guessing with Hank. If he didn't like something in your book, you were not only made aware of it but told why. He had this boisterous but genuine friendly thing about him that made you like him right away. Just as I was about to leave his office with my tail between my legs, he blurted out that he thought I had a lot of talent and wanted me to have an interview with the creative director, William Free.

William Free was this very impressive looking gentleman who looked like he bought all his clothes at Harrods in London. Unfortunately, he had enough dandruff on his jacket to bread a veal cutlet, and he had these white fungus looking things growing around his eyes. I couldn't look anywhere else but right at them. I was sure he knew it!

He thumbed through my book without saying a word and then looked up at me and said, "When can you start?"

I felt sort of disloyal to Y&R, which up until now was like home to me, but I guess even the most timid of birds has to leave the nest at some point.

I went from a piddly salary of $125 a week to a whopping salary of $160 in one jump. I was so excited! I was getting closer to my lifetime goal of making $10,000 a year.

I was thankful to Jeff Metzner for telling me about this incredible opportunity, but I was not exactly enamored with having to share an office with him. It was pressure enough to be working in this creative hot shop without having to be compared to the talent and persona of this wonderful wild man!

Up and down the halls of Marschalk were writers and art directors who were in the process of making names for themselves. People like Tony Mandarino, Art Hawkins, Bill McCaffrey, Hank Seiden, Bill Free, Marcella Free, and Marvin Mitchnick. They were all on the cutting edge of advertising at the time, and there I was feeling like I had somehow slipped in under the door when no one was looking.

If you needed answers or direction for something you were working on, all you had to do was pop into any office at any time of day (or night I might add) to get a powerful critique. Nobody pulled any punches either, and I think that I appreciated that the most.

I remember Marvin Mitchnick frantically creating way-out layouts for Contadina Tomato Sauce and Chung King Chinese Food. He wielded his rubber cement brush like he was making some wild abstract painting. He was actually turning the design page into a form of collage, and there were times when the page began to take on size and dimension. When he was finished, there was rubber cement everywhere, but he was creating unusual breakthrough stuff at the same time. Watching him work, taking chances, helped me to break out of my conservative mold.

Then there was Tony Mandarino, another wild man of sorts who had a way of jolting you with a visual. He did this ad for Fram Filters, and instead of seeing the traditional three-quarter view of an automobile with the hood open, which made perfectly good sense, he created this double-page spread looking at the under-carriage of the car. It was startling, powerful, and there was no way that you could turn the page without paying attention to it.

Tony was the character of characters. I remember him throwing an account executive out of his office bodily one day and then laughing hysterically about it later. It was always Tony against the suits. He never liked account people, and he looked at them as vipers in grey flannel suits whose only job was to bring an ad down to its most boring level.

Not possessing the same fire as Tony, I found my own way to get around the suits. After designing my ads, I would render them into comprehensive finished layouts and then stick them into my drawer. I would then invite the account executive into my office and show him my rough layouts, thereby including him in the creative process. The suits always walked away from my office thinking that they had some input into creating the ad. Now, instead of having an adversary, I had a partner.

Then there was Bill McCaffrey. He was this incredibly articulate, gentle man who took great pride in bringing along the young designers at the agency. We used to gather around him as though we were going to hear the Sermon on the Mount. He loved typography, and he opened my eyes to the personality that each and every typeface was imbued with.

Marschalk in the early sixties was a great place for a young art director to be honing his design skills, and not only that but, because the agency had a reputation for doing breakthrough work, the headhunters were constantly at the door with job opportunities.

The late fifties and early sixties were the beginning of the creative revolution in the advertising business. Although none of us realized that we were in a revolution at the time, you couldn't help but be excited about the quality of the work that was popping up all over the city.

George Lois (of Lois, Holland, and Callaway) did a wonderful advertisement for Harvey Probber Chairs, which showed a simple visual of a chair in the middle of the floor with a match pack stuck underneath one of the legs, and read, "If a Harvey Probber Chair wobbles, straighten the floor."

George single-handedly gave credence to the art director as a conceptual person. Up until then, most art directors pushed around graphics elements to make a page look good, but most of the real thinking was credited to the writer.

George somehow brought a certain kind of Bronx street smarts to Madison Avenue and turned it into sophisticated and powerful images that wed themselves to the copy perfectly. The copy without the visual was of no effect and vice-versa.

I obtained a wonderful visual device from George Lois that I still use to this day when teaching young students. A simple change can make a huge difference in the graphic communication for an advertisement.

The ad starts out with an ordinary square halftone with a headline and body copy below. The visual is a bottle of children's cough syrup with the headline that reads in large letters, "Tastes Good."

The students always pause and look at me with quizzical looks on their faces as if to say, "Has he lost his marbles... What is interesting about that?" Then I go back to the blackboard and add two straws with candy red stripes to the bottle, and suddenly their frowns turn to smiles. The addition of the straws turns something ordinary into something extraordinary.

The Marschalk experience did much to open me up. I did some award-winning ads for 4711 Eau de Cologne and Schrafft's Ice Cream, and the headhunters began knocking at my door.

I went on a few interviews just to test the waters. I went to see an art director by the name of Louis Musachio at Papert Koenig and Lois. PKL, as they were called. Their agency was on fire, and just getting an interview there was a huge compliment.

Louis Musachio was this five-foot-something little dynamo who smoked cigars that were just a little bit shorter than he was.

As he looked at my book through a cloud of smoke, he paused at everything that wasn't pure advertising and said, "Get this shit out of your book. Do you want to be a designer, an illustrator, or an advertising art director? This shit has got to go."

I was so much in awe of him and the agency that I couldn't say a word. In those days art directors that were winning awards, guys who had names were like rock stars. I remember going to photographers' parties and standing in the corner saying, "Look, there's Peter Hirsch, and who is that guy with him in the white suit?

Wow… That's Jerry Andriozzi."

Then I went on an interview with one of the best-known art directors in the business by the name of Onofrio Paccione. He actually loved my book, and right there on the spot offered me a job for ten thousand dollars a year. I was blown away. My lifetime goal was offered to me, just like that.

I went back to Marschalk and immediately into Hank Seiden's office. "Are you crazy, kid?" he yelled. "You are working for the hottest agency in town right now. Sit down. I'll talk to Bill…and don't move until I get back."

I sat there for about an hour, literally twiddling my thumbs when Hank came back into the room. "Bill will go for twelve thousand … you owe me. Now get the hell out of here," he said with a laugh.

My wife was at her mother's house that night, and I went straight there for her usual Thursday night dinner—which included mashed potatoes with butter, string beans in garlic vinegar, and well done roast beef, very well done.

"I have an announcement to make," I said.

My mother-in-law looked over at my wife, who had recently given birth to our second son within fifteen months of the first. "No, not again… So soon!"

"You all remember that my goal in life was to make ten thousand dollars a year?"

"Yes," answered my mother-in-law, relieved that her daughter wasn't pregnant again.

"Well, it's never going to happen... They just bumped me up from eight thousand dollars a year to twelve thousand in one shot."

The room went silent. They had never heard of numbers like that in their entire lives.

I must tell you it was a little difficult to call Onofrio Paccione the next day to tell him I wasn't coming because I kind of...well, sort of...accepted the job on the spot. He was very good about it, however, and let me off the hook!

To celebrate, I went out and bought a new Buick Riviera. Man, what a beauty. It was a champagne color with a saddle interior, had a cool-looking wooden knob on the shift and headlights that opened and closed, revealing the lights within!

My mother wanted to kill me.

"You have a family to take care of... You make a little money, and you throw it away on a car?"

I chalked it up to her having barely made it through the Depression and continued to drool over my car!

That Buick looked awesome sitting in the driveway of our little house in Bloomfield, New Jersey.

We bought the house for $20,400 only a matter of months before while I was still at the staggering salary of $160 a week. Then we were hit with having to replace the front steps and the boiler at the same time. We borrowed $400 from my mother and $400 from our children's bank account.

I must say it was a little scary, but the new salary changed everything. In retrospect, I guess I can understand my mother's concern about the car.

After about two years at Marschalk, I worked my way up to Senior Art Director and a salary of about $15,000, and the headhunters were beginning to pitch tents in the agency lobby.

It was around Christmastime, and the whole creative department was asked to work on what they called a "push." That meant a client was making threatening noises about moving on, and everyone had to make a huge effort to keep his business. That meant working around the clock, presenting our wares up and down the halls—from the account people to the creative supervisor to the creative director and then to the plans board. If your ad made it through that without looking like chopped liver, you were good!

This particular push was for the Gorham Silver account, and I must say my work made it through with the plans board's approval pending the president of the agency, Stewart Watson's anointing.

We gathered up our work at about 9:30 pm, which by now was in its final stages, and proceeded to the boardroom for the final head-nod from The Pres.

He hated it and not only ordered us back to the drawing board but wanted to know how the plans board could have let it get this far in the first place. No one took responsibility for having approved our work. In fact, there were some utterances to the effect that this stuff only came down the pike at the last minute.

I sat there for a while, smoke beginning to billow from my ears, waiting for someone on the plans board to have the balls enough to admit that they were equally responsible for the state that we were in.

Finally, I stood up and spewed, "I can't believe what I'm seeing here. You all approved this stuff, and now you're acting like you had nothing to do with it!"

No one even had testicles big enough to refute me or shut me up! Finally, Hank Seiden stood up and said, "The kid is right. We all played a part in this."

"That's neither here nor there," said Mr. Watson. "The meeting is tomorrow, and we can't waste time discussing who shot who," and stomped out of the boardroom.

I was fuming! If it wasn't bad enough that I had an all-nighter staring me in the face, I was feeling violated at the same time.

We had a short meeting in Bill Free's office and were all sent our ways to finish a completely new presentation.

I sat in front of my drawing board—tired, disgusted, and downright angry!

I called my wife and told her what had happened and said that I was thinking of quitting on the spot and could she support me in that. God love her, she said that she was totally behind me in whatever decision that I made.

I picked myself up and walked into Bill Free's office, who was there talking with Hank Seiden. Before I could even get a word out, Hank jumped up, "I can see it all over your face; don't say a word."

With that, he walked me around the entire agency arm in arm, in an effort to talk some sense into me. I finally calmed down and went back to my office. I sat once again in front of my drawing board, staring at the blank drawing pad.

I couldn't do it! I just could not … do it! I went back into Bill's office again. Hank said, "Don't say…"

Bill said, "No, let the kid talk."

"I quit!" I said, and left!

Well, integrity had its way with me that night, and as soon as I hit the cold air, it struck me that this was Christmastime, and no one looks for a job at Christmas.

That was the longest and coldest bus ride home of my life.

The next morning I was gathering my things together when Bill Free burst into my office, "I want you out of here by noon!" and left in a cloud of dandruff. I think he got that line from an old western that he had seen the night before. My friends Vince Daddiego, Joe DeVoto, and John Baeder all stopped in to give their condolences. Joey blurted out as only he could, "Where the 'F' are you going?" he said. "I just 'F'ing got here and you're 'F'ing going? You gotta' be 'F'ing kidding me."

Incredible as it may seem, thanks to Judy Wald—the headhunter extraordinaire, I got a job before the week was up.

Dick Calderhead, the man I shared the supply room with at Young & Rubicam during the summer of '59, had just been hired as the creative director of the Campbell-Ewald agency and thought enough of me to bring me in from the cold. It wasn't exactly the kind of creative shop that I had been used to for the last few years, but I knew Dick to be a very good creative person, and he was hired to turn the place around. The challenge was exciting, and I would be right there in the thick of it.

Not more than two weeks went by when I got a phone call from a friend of mine by the name of Dick Singer. He had interviewed at a really hot creative shop called Delahanty, Kurnit & Geller. He said they were completely restructuring the place and that there were a couple of jobs for young art directors. He was convinced that he was one of them and he wanted me to go with him.

That was really thoughtful of him, but I said that really wouldn't be right, seeing as I just started here and

Dick being a friend and all.

"Are you kidding me?" he said. "Dick went up for the job himself!"

I marched right into Calderhead's office, "You just hired me, and you're off on an interview at DKG?"

"Look, I'm sorry, but the opportunity came up, and I owed it to myself to check it out."

"What about the idea of turning this place into a hot shop ... was that all a figment of your imagination?"

"Look," he said, "I didn't get the job, so you give it a try. If you get it, so be it. And if you don't, come back here and we'll start all over again."

Well, I did go for it, and I got it. Unfortunately, there really was only one job open for a young art director, and Dick Singer, out of his thoughtfulness and kindness, screwed himself out of the job. I felt bad, but he was a real mensch about it all.

DKG ... This Is Huge!

Every time I moved up the ladder, I had the feeling that I was in over my head ... and I was, but you know something, you get to be a better swimmer that way.

Not only was I working in perhaps one of the most creative hot shops at the time, but they kicked my salary up to $18,000 a year.

We're talking about some heavy hitters here.

Peter Hirsch, one of the best art directors in the business, was the head art director and would continue in that job, and this crazy Italian copywriter by the name of Jerry Della Femina was brought in as the creative director. There were a bunch of young gonna-be-superstars there also, like Dick Raboy, Frank Siebke, Stu Hyatt, and little ol' me, just to name a few.

Shep Kurnit was the owner. Somehow Delehanty and Geller had faded away into the advertising sunset. Shep was a visionary with a car salesman's personality. He truly knew talent when he saw it, but unfortunately wasn't sure how to support them to do their best work. Sometimes, and I'm being polite here, he would put a headlock on the creative necks of the people he was paying a lot of money to produce for him.

I remember Stu Hyatt was about to go into a meeting to present a campaign to one of our clients, and Shep asked to see the copy before the client saw it. Stu looked Shep right in the face, pointed to his own head, and said, "The copy is all right here in my head where you can't change it."

Shep was one of a kind. As I said before, he had this creative thing going on the inside, and this car salesman's persona going on the outside. It was a very strange combination, to say the least. He used to talk to you with his face only two or three inches away from yours, and when he got excited, he would kind of spit on you. I remember Jerry Della Femina would always wait for Shep to move in close for one of his speech baths, and then Jerry would immediately light a cigarette holding the lit match like a torch forcing Shep to take a step backward.

Talon Zippers was one of the accounts that gave the agency the opportunity to execute strong creative work. I remember this one ad that simply showed a close-up of a man looking at a note that obviously had just been handed to him. The note read, "Your fly is open."

Talon came out with a nylon zipper that they ended up calling The Talon Nylon Zephyr Zipper. The main benefit was its continuous nylon coil configuration, which made it far superior to the metal zipper. The metal zipper had individual teeth, each sewn into the fabric, which meant that they could pull out ruining the entire zipper. Whereas the nylon coil was one piece, and the teeth could not pull out. The second benefit of the Talon Zipper was that the color was fused into the plastic, and it could be matched to the color of the garment. Another benefit was that it could never fade or chip like the painted metal zippers.

I did this extravagant ad take-off on *The Wizard of Oz* showing Dorothy, the Lion, the Scarecrow, the Tin Man, and Toto walking the yellow brick road with the headline, "We finally found a guy who looks good in a metal zipper."

It was the first good ad that I did there and kept me from being fired. Up until then, I had done some fairly ordinary stuff, and I sensed that my head was ready for the chopping block. Shep was not one to wait around for you to "develop." He was a quick study, and I knew I was in trouble because his brother-in-law/business manager kept sticking his head in my office with this shit-eating-grin saying, "How you doing?"

I found out later that Shep indeed threatened to let me go. But I was saved by Jerry Della Femina, who squared off with him saying, "If the kid goes, I go … give him a chance."

I never forgot that bold move on Jerry's part, especially since Fran had just given birth to our third son. Needless to say, I was indebted to Jerry for that courageous support.

Thank God, I began to do some award-winning work, I mean Jerry could only back me up just so long.

I did this ad, which became a classic. I did a take-off

on a Peanuts cartoon by Charles M. Shultz, where I showed a kid on the pitcher's mound with the catcher making his way to the mound to talk to him. He had thinking balloons over his head saying things like, "What's he coming out here for … he gonna' say something to rattle me … I know he's gonna say something like, 'your fastball is losing its zip' … I just know he's gonna say something to rattle me."

The catcher finally makes his way up to the pitcher and says, "Your fly is open." At the bottom of the ad was a logo line that read Talon Zipper with memory lock, the zipper that always remembers to stay up.

I originally wanted Charles Shultz to draw the cartoon, but he rejected it. Frustrated, I finished the ad in photography and even went as far as to have shirts made up like the Peanut's characters.

The ad ran its course. We got a cease and desist order from Shultz, so we had to pull the ad, but by that time, we had accomplished what we wanted.

I won all kinds of awards for that ad, but one of the most embarrassing things in my life also happened with that ad at the Art Directors Show of New York. We were at the awards dinner, and the word was out that I had won the gold medal for the Peanuts Ad in the trade category. It was a lock. I was so confident that I had won that I wasn't even nervous about it.

Then came the time for the gold medal to be

announced. Everyone at the table gave me the thumbs up. I even adjusted my chair so that I would have easy access to the center aisle. The announcer said, "In the category of trade ads, the award … goes to … Ron… Well, I was up and out of my seat faster than a jack-rabbit, and then he finished the sentence. Ron… Ron Brillo!

There was nowhere to hide. I couldn't fake that I was on my way to the bathroom or anything, so I just sheepishly backed myself up into my chair and stared at the floor for the rest of the evening. I did manage to get an honorable mention, however, but that just didn't cut it, if you know what I mean!

Jerry was a terrific creative director. He created the perfect atmosphere for doing good award-winning work, and when Shep would jump in to mucky up an ad, Jerry would act as a buffer zone.

Jerry would set Shep up as the bad guy, which wasn't all that hard to do, and then the entire creative team would rally around Jerry for support! It was a brilliant strategy.

On another occasion, we were working late putting together a new business creative presentation for a company called Liteolear. We had a bunch of their lamps to use as props for our presentation. Under Shep's instructions, I plugged one of the lights into a socket, and all the lights in the office suddenly went out.

"What the hell did you do?" said Shep in his inimitable way.

I then looked out the window, and the lights all over the city began to go out, block after block as though God had suddenly decided to pull the plug on us all.

"Holy Shit!" said Shep, "What the f_ _ _ have you done?"

It turns out, it was November 9, 1965, and we were experiencing the most incredible blackout the city has ever known. It was the strangest experience of my life. To see a city the size of New York in total darkness was a mind-blower. The only lights you could see were from the cars below that were beginning to stack up because all the streetlights and traffic lights went as well.

I heard screaming coming from the lobby. People were stuck between floors in the elevators.

"Help! ... Help! What's going on? We're stuck in the elevator, and it is pitch black in here!" cried a woman looking for some encouragement that her life wasn't coming to a quick and nasty end.

"Hold on, the electricity is out," I said in an effort to comfort her.

"Oh... Thank God, somebody must have blown a fuse or something, huh?"

Without thinking it out, I said, "No, the lights went out all over the city. We don't know what is going on."

Then she really panicked, "Oh my Lord... Oh my

Lord…Lordy…Lordy… Somebody get me out of here!" she screamed.

The elevators were designed in such a manner that the car finally leveled off at our floor, and we somehow managed to pry open the doors.

What a night! People ended up sleeping on the floors of their offices and drinking the night away in candle-lit bars and restaurants. They say more babies were born nine months later than at any other time in history. I said before that we were in a creative revolution … but this was creativity on another level.

In most businesses, if you had more than a few jobs on your resume, you were looked at as someone who was a bit irresponsible. That was not true of the advertising business, however. In fact, if one was to spend an inordinate span of time with one organization, that person would be looked upon as someone who was too conservative and perhaps not an exciting and powerful creative person.

As I said before, this was the '60s, and we were actually defining the creative revolution. It wasn't long before we all were being offered spectacular jobs almost every day!

Who Bates Who?

Four of us were offered huge jobs at the Ted Bates ad agency, and *The Wall Street Journal* deemed it important enough to write an article on its front page entitled, "The Rich Kids."

Jerry was offered $50,000 a year, and the rest of us were offered $30,000. This was outstanding money in those days, and we moved on it at the speed of light with the expressed idea that we would springboard into our own agency within a year.

We were guns for hire, and the Ted Bates people immediately housed us in a hidden corner of the agency so that we couldn't infect the rest of the agency with this creative stuff. They didn't really want us, but they needed to be able to tell their clients that they had some of these revolutionary creative weirdos.

They would open the door once in a while and throw in a piece of meat and then quickly shut the door behind them. They really didn't want us to associate with their regular staff because we wanted things like the ability to present our own work to the clients, and that was unheard of.

"You mean you guys sell your own work?" one of the art directors said to me. "You're actually allowed to go to the production shoot of your commercial? We have to turn it all over to a producer. We never see it again until it is finished."

I felt like I was working in some darkened mine-shaft waiting for the canary to die.

The first day I joined the company, I went to my new office, put my jacket over the back of my chair, and left for the Upper Montclair Country Club to watch the new golf sensation Jack Nicklaus play in the Thunderbird Golf Tournament.

While I was at Bates, I taught design classes at The School of Visual Arts, had a freelance job, and produced more work at the agency than any art director there.

This company was so big and unruly that there was a writer who actually held a position at Ted Bates and Benton & Bowles at the same time. He would present himself at Bates in the morning, go down the elevator, and up to Benton & Bowles on the other side of the building. He managed to get away with it until the two creative directors had lunch together one day.

It was at Ted Bates that Jerry Della Femina made his now-famous remark at the first meeting of the Creative Review Board (I use that term loosely) for their newly acquired account, Panasonic. They wanted to impress the new client with their new creative geniuses.

In the very first meeting, Jerry raised his hand, paused for a second, and said, "I have it. I have the new line for the Panasonic Company."

Everyone in the room came to an abrupt halt waiting

to hear what this new highly paid genius was going to say, and Jerry spit out, "Panasonic… From those wonderful folks who gave you Pearl Harbor."

Lit pipes began dropping out of the mouths of the suits all over the conference table. While their attention was consumed with collecting the ashes before they burned holes in the shiny oak table, we escaped and went back to our creative cages.

To this day, I have no idea whether they thought that was a real concept, or if hiring Jerry and his band of creative cuckoos was the worst idea the agency ever had.

All I know was that working at Bates that year was one of the all-time great experiences of my advertising career.

Up until that point, I wasn't much of a drinker, but lunchtime became a wonderful training program. We thought nothing of having two or three Tanqueray Martini's on the rocks with three olives.

Not only did we do more work than any other group in the agency, but we also did it in less time and with the best record of selling the work to the clients.

With my salary, the freelancing, and the teaching, I made close to $60,000 that year, enough to buy three Buick Rivieras. I told my mom. Her eyes rolled back in her head with the thought that I might be dumb enough to actually do something as stupid as that.

The year was 1966, and color television was beginning

to catch on. The first ad we did for Panasonic's introduction to their color TV business came right out of real consideration for prospective buyers into this new arena. The headline was, "Are you afraid your first color television will turn out to be a $600.00 dog?"

That had to get your attention if you were considering buying one of these expensive experiments. It was a powerful selling device because it was telling the truth, which I might add was usually at the center of most good advertisements.

After a while, they had us working every account that seemed to be having a problem. We were asked to come up with a mnemonic device (that's a memorable device) for the 3 Musketeers Candy Bar.

We had this idea of having the sound effects of the Three Musketeers riding their horses within the package itself, yelling out, "One for all and all for one." Let's face it, it wasn't a very good idea in the first place, but when Jerry put on his "production hat" it really got ridiculous.

He suggested we build a huge candy bar with gears in it to give it movement while we dubbed in the sound effects and dialogue. This was a demonstration commercial, mind you, one that needed to be tested before the actual commercial would be produced. The cost to produce Jerry's idea would have been ludicrous to say nothing about the ridiculous gymnastics we'd have to go through to put such a thing together.

So we mounted a real candy bar to a blackboard, cut a hole in the back of the board, and like a puppeteer, allowed our fingers to do the movement.

There is no question that Jerry is a brilliant man, but when it came to production, we always had to turn a deaf ear.

"Hit the Sign ... Win a Suit!"

Anyone who ever watched a game at Ebbets Field remembers the sign in right field that read, "Hit the sign ... Win a suit!"—created and paid for by the clothing storeowner Abe Stark. Not only was it a brilliant concept creatively speaking, but a brilliant media buy as well. What made it even more wonderful was that no one could ever hit that sign without killing the right fielder first.

I love the power of the printed word. Great advertising, especially great print advertising, always came close to being fine art for me. The idea of putting a headline and a graphic together and motivating someone to act on the message blows me away.

A powerful advertisement actually includes the viewer in the creative process. When they get your communication, they feel smart and think you are smart for creating it. When that process is too slow, they get turned off and think you're a dummy for creating such drivel.

Sometimes the visual and the headline are one and the same. I remember a couple of ads done by Dick Lopez that were brilliant and motivating with a well-placed well-written headline only.

He did an ad for The Holy Name Society. It was a full-page ad with a black background and in extremely bold, huge white typeface, which read, "Jesus Christ." There is no way you can turn that page, whether you were a believer or not. At the bottom of the page, it read in smaller letters, "This can be said in prayer or in anger. The Holy Name Society needs you to keep it in prayer. Join."

Dick created a wonderful public service subway poster, which spoke to the importance of staying in school. Once again the power of this headline needed no visual. It read, "I quit school when I were sixteen."

Then there was the brilliant advertising campaign for Volkswagen's Beetle, in the face of a world that was enamored with large automobiles, they ran ads that said things like, "Think small."

Most great advertising comes out of the truth... Now I didn't say that most advertising tells the truth; what I said was that the technique of interesting someone in what it is that you have to say very often comes out of a true experience.

I remember an ad campaign for Horn & Hardart created by Ron Barrett and Ed McCabe that told the truth about the good food but also took liberty with the fact that their restaurants weren't known for their elegant surroundings. The campaign theme was, "Horn & Hardart, You can't eat atmosphere." Brilliant!

Bob Gill, the famous illustrator/graphic designer, once used a teaching example that drives home the point of using words and graphics that come out of some truism.

He had been given an assignment to create an announcement for The Forum Gallery that was moving to a new location. Instead of doing the obvious, Bob showed how using something out of a real-life experience would make a more memorable image.

We have all experienced at one time or another that removing a painting, which had been hanging on a wall for some time, would leave a discoloration where the picture had been. So Bob designed an off-white page with an even whiter area where the painting had been hanging. He also put a nail hole at the top. The headline simply read, "The Forum Art Gallery has moved."

In the rent-a-car business where Hertz controlled the market hands down, Avis was fighting for second place with National Car Rental. They created a theme that they would use for the next 50 years: "Avis. We Try Harder." This was not so much an attempt to take away business necessarily from Hertz, but to position themselves clearly as the second choice, thereby leaping over National.

That kind of marketing thinking and brilliant creativity truly gets me excited.

In my own company, we brought Beck's Beer, which was importing only 50,000 cases a year into the American market, to over 500,000 cases of beer in less than a year with a simple concept, "When you think of beer what country do you think of … then shouldn't you be drinking the beer that sells best in that country? Beck's … the number one best-selling beer in Germany!"

That was the marketing strategy and creative at the same time. We also maximized their budget by running ten-second commercials with that message, and rolled out market by market, ending up with a huge success story!

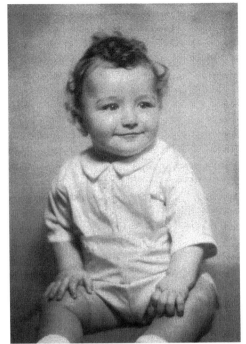

Top Row: Phyllis Travisano (Mom), me at age 1, Biagio (Ben) Travisano (Dad)
Bottom: My sister Laura, Dad, and me; Mom and me on the beach

Left to Right, Top to Bottom: Me in a rabbit costume made by my mother; My oldest friends Chuck Mazzeo (front) and Mike Sprague; Me with my dog Snuffy; My best friend at Carteret Prep, Matt Palmieri; The Jersey Shore (all departed but me)

Three shots of me in the U.S. Army, and one of Mark Yustein **(lower right)** before he proved that the pen was mightier than the bazooka

Lower Left: My future wife Fran Bongiovanni and me at age 19
Top and Right: Our wedding day, June 10, 1961

Top: What I looked like when Jerry Della Femina and I started the agency

Middle Row: The original "Mad Men" (Jerry far left, and upper right respectively)

Bottom: The first office photo

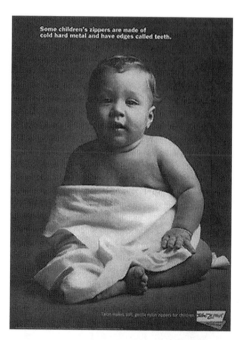

Top: Tin Man, Talon Zippers print ad
Bottom: Award-winning print ad created with Mark Yustein for Channel 7 Eyewitness News

Top: Talon Zippers print ad featuring my son Vincent
Bottom: Print ad created with Ellen Simons for Jaquet Cosmetics

Left: Meow Mix—the most memorable TV commercial ever, and winner of a Clio Award
Middle: Award-winning "Peanuts" Talon Zippers print ad; Corum Watch print ad
Bottom: Some of my advertising awards;
A frame from an Isuzu TV commercial that won an award at the Cannes Film Festival

Left to Right, Top to Bottom: Art Director cousin Vincent DiGiacomo, the one who sparked it all; Me with Herschel Levit; Creating an ad in my office (Mark Yustein and Neil Drossman to the right of me); Me, Phil Suarez, and George Lois **(Left to Right)**

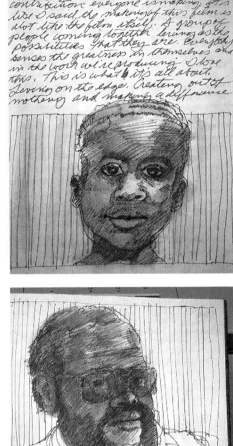

Sketches and notes while filming "Africa the Possibility"

Top and Middle: Crew and cast of *Africa the Possibility*
Right: The star of the film and me

Final Mel Brooks Teacher's Scotch print ad created by Nick Gisonde and Neil Drossman; On the set of "Young Frankenstein"; Mel dressed for his tuxedo idea (I am still waiting for the case of scotch.)

Opposite Page: With comic legends Dom DeLuise (for a Ziploc Bags commercial), Redd Foxx, and George Burns (both for Teacher's Scotch print ads)

This Page: With authors Hal Lindsey, and Ayn Rand (for a Daily News ad); With actor Paul Newman (producing a commercial for a Japanese production company)

With actor James Earl Jones (on a Yellow Pages commercial shoot).
With actress/comedian Whoopi Goldberg (for an MCI commercial).

With sports legends Greg Norman and Joe Torre. "Time to make the donuts" with actor Michael Vale

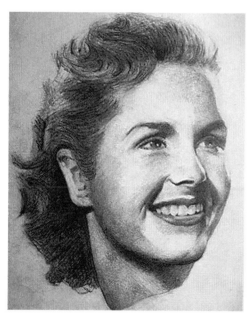

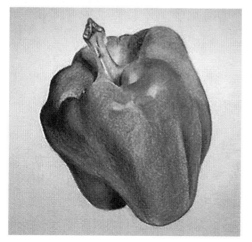

Left to Right, Top to Bottom: Debbie Reynolds drawing done at age 17; Marlon Brando painting done as an adult; Rhino drawing; Drawing of a bust done at age 14; Drawing of a bell pepper

Top to Bottom: Watercolor painting of an Italian reading a newspaper; Watercolor of an old woman sleeping at St. Peter's Basilica in Rome; Posing with my favorite self-portrait at an art exhibit

I am the God of my Universe

I have wings, and I was meant to fly...so what!

What I have been withholding is... I love you

The one who ends up with the most cheese is the winner!

My philosophy of life is... do it to them before they do it to you!

I find it easier to ride the person in the direction they're going.

Above: EST-themed cartoons for a book project. **Below:** Small dog watercolor series. **Bottom:** First watercolor done at age 14

Clockwise from Top Left:
Portrait of my children Ronald and
Laura; Portrait of my wife Fran;
Self-portrait; A rare landscape
depicting Upstate New York

Top to Bottom: Portrait of friend Barbara; A friend who resembles Vincent van Gogh, and my portrait of him in the style of Van Gogh; Portraits of friend Bob Garofalo and of his daughter Gabrielle

Top Right: My father Ben doing a wood carving. **Other Shots This Page:** Various animal wood carvings, an art I picked up from my father whose carving tools I still use. Later on in life I learned that my family in Italy were wood carvers.

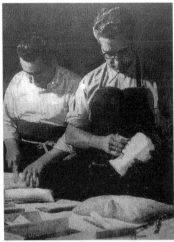

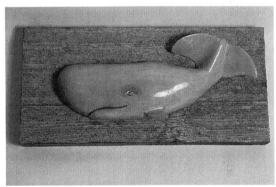

Opposite Page, Top to Bottom, Left to Right: American Flag and George Washington; Illustration on newspaper; AdVets for WarVets; Portrait of migrant worker; AdVets for WarVets

This Page, Top to Bottom: My 80th birthday celebration in Tuscany, Italy including my four children, their spouses, grandchildren, local friends, and my girlfriend Nina Neglia; Four generations of Travisanos including my father Ben, my son Vincent, his son Paul, and myself; An ad for my free graphic design class held at my condo

Part 4

Della Femina, Travisano, Tolmach & Siebke?

One year to the day, on October 10th, 1967, we left Ted Bates and started our own advertising agency in a suite at the Gotham Hotel. We agreed to call the agency Jerry Della Femina & Partners because there is no way to put those four names together and make it memorable. Anyway, Jerry was the most famous member of the group, and we thought it best to take advantage of that.

We managed somehow to put together about one hundred thousand dollars in backing from friends and relatives. None of us really knew anything about the business of business or even how to go about renting office space. Most of us had never been in a meeting with a client. We certainly had no idea how to go about pitching new business. Although we were very well known for being creative print mavens, none of us had much experience producing TV commercials.

It was with that experience and knowledge that we launched our ship into the turbulent seas of advertising.

I have often said in motivational speeches that I've been privileged to make, "If we ever knew what we didn't know, we would never have done it. Thank God, we didn't know what we didn't know."

We found space, 2,300 square feet, to be exact, at 635 Madison on the 8th floor. That alone was very exciting. We hired a lady by the name of Barbara Kalish (who was our "gal everything") and a print production manager by the name of Ray Greiche.

We were in business! Of course, we didn't have any business, but as long as the hundred thousand held out, we were in business.

Jerry had worked on a freelance account while at Bates called Squire Hairpieces for Men, and although it didn't pay very much, it was our first piece of business.

We were making presentations every day, sometimes several a day. I remember one afternoon getting to one address after having presented two other times that morning, and I couldn't remember what kind of a company it was. I leaned over to Jerry and said, "Who are we pitching … I can't remember." He refused to tell me. He got the biggest bang out of my suffering.

What was wonderful about those early days was that we were a bunch of kids with nothing to lose and everything to gain. I was 29, Jerry was 30, Ned Tolmach was 30, and Frank Siebke was about 32.

I once said to Jerry, "If we ever get to a place where we have everything to lose and nothing to gain, I am out of here."

Well, a few months went by, and although we had some inroads to accounts that seemed to like what we had to say, the money in the bank was getting rather low, so low that Frank and Ned decided after a very long lunch that they wanted out.

Jerry and I couldn't believe it, and as we walked sadly up 56th Street, Jerry turned to me and said, "What about you?" I said without hesitation, "I am in all the way. If I have to sell my house and move in with my wife's parents, then that is what I'll have to do."

It was at that very moment that Jerry and I truly started the agency. It was out of that commitment that the context for success was created.

We were getting kind of close to bottom when the bank statement showed that we actually only had about four thousand dollars left. My wife had just given birth to our fourth child, a beautiful little girl, and things were getting tight in every way.

While Frank and Ned were doing whatever they had to do to extricate themselves from us, we found out that a few accounts that we had been pitching were about to anoint us with their business. Moxie Soda, American Home Assurance Company, and a beauty shop supply company all came in at the same time.

Jerry said to me, "We should throw a party and announce all this business at once, and everyone will think we're doing great." I said, "Are you crazy? We have four thousand dollars left, and you want to throw a party... What the hell, let's do it!"

We had the party, the publicity was incredible, and word spread like wildfire that we were doing wonderfully. Ha!

The "Ins" and the "Outs"

That was the backbone of our financial system, as long as the "ins" were more than the "outs"—we would be fine. We actually did our financial reports every week on the back of manila envelopes. In fact, years later, when the agency was a true success, I had one of those envelopes framed and gave it to Jerry for Christmas.

Little by little, we grew, and by the end of the year, we actually picked up our first million-dollar account, Schieffelin & Co., with products like Blue Nun Wine, Ruffino Wine, and Tio Pepe. We were beside ourselves. No one can ever explain the excitement that goes along with sticking your neck out and then finally succeeding.

I remember calling my mother ten minutes after we heard the news. "Mom… It's me. Guess what? We picked up our first one-million-dollar account. We're a success!"

"Don't count your chickens before they hatch," she said.

Don't get me wrong; she was a great mom. But as I said before, most of the parents who lived through the Great Depression and the Second World War came out a little shell-shocked, and I believe they found it difficult to throw around compliments. I think they thought it might place some kind of curse on you if you actually enjoyed something.

My mom was an incredibly bright woman, and obviously her approval meant a lot to me, but sharing a success story with her wasn't the way to get it.

She also had a very good sense of humor, and you had to keep your ears and heart open because her compliments had a way of slipping in without you realizing it. Sometimes she would say the opposite of what you wanted to hear and then give you a big smile. You were supposed to get the meaning behind the meaning.

For example, I wanted to actually hear her say to me, "I love you," and her response was, "I hate you," ... smile!

"No, really, Mom, just once I want to hear you say, "I love you."

"I hate you," she repeated once again with a huge smile.

Then many years later, she began to suffer from Alzheimer's disease, and although she got to a point that she could hardly remember who I was, somehow her sense of humor remained intact.

I went to visit her at the assisted living home and played Scrabble with her, which by the way, she loved beating the crap out of everyone she played—she was so very competitive.

Anyway, we were playing, and this woman (who was farther along in her Alzheimer's experience than my mom) was walking around the table babbling away as though she was instructing us on how to play the game.

My mom put her head down and was busily moving tiles around on her tray, then turned the tray towards me with a maniacal smile on her face, which read, "Shut up!" Incredible!

One day she was found on the floor of her room and was taken to the hospital. My sister and I got a call, and we rushed up there to support her.

They had her in the emergency room on a gurney for hours putting her through one test after another, which by the way, turned out to be nothing more than dehydration.

My sister and I stood by her side for at least five hours. At one point, my mom became very irritated and said, "Why am I here? What am I doing here? What is going on?"

My sister tried to calm her down. She tenderly touched her arm and said, "Mother ... you must try to keep your wits about you."

She looked at the two of us and said, "I only have two half-wits, and they are both here."

Our laughing caused a ruckus in the emergency room.

To this day, I have never been able to understand how her mind could seemingly be dissolving in every area of her life but not her sense of humor.

From Those Wonderful Folks Who Gave You Pearl Harbor

It was during that first year that Jerry wrote his best-selling book, *From Those Wonderful Folks Who Gave You Pearl Harbor.*

As much as his newfound fame helped grow our agency, that's how bad it was for deflating my ego. Up until then, I was able to keep whatever insecurities I had at bay with compliments about my artistic talents and reasonable good looks.

With all this new success, the money started to roll in. Success breeds success, and I started to collect toys with the idea that the more toys I had, the more satisfaction I would experience.

And as much as I am embarrassed to admit it, I began to collect relationships with women as well. I guess power and success are attractive, and like some rock star riding his success into the sewer, I went with the flow. My need for self-esteem took a wrong turn for sure!

I went out one day at lunch and bought a brand new Jaguar XKE V-12 convertible. It was racing-car green with a saddle interior, and I figured anyone seeing me in it would be green with envy.

"I'd like to drive this home today… Can you make that happen?" I said firmly to the shiny haired salesman.

"Certainly, Mr. Travisano," he said, rubbing his

hands together as though he had just met a live one.

I went right to the bank, wrote out a check for the full value of the car, and was driving that baby home before the sun went down.

The only problem… I was no more than a block away when I realized that I really didn't want this speed-mobile that could go from zero to sixty in four seconds flat. I couldn't even fit in the thing comfortably. To make matters even worse, on the way home—the engine froze, and the car died in the middle of the Lincoln Tunnel.

This satisfaction that I was seeking was only lasting a little more than a few blocks. Down and down I went, not loving that spin I was in.

Now that Ned and Frank had left, there were just the two of us remaining. There was no reason to only have Jerry's name on the masthead. So, to help boost my image, and to get my mother off my back about the single name on the masthead, we changed the name of the agency to Della Femina, Travisano & Partners—and that definitely helped … for a while.

I used to sit in meetings wondering why people were only looking at Jerry. Even when I would ask a question, they would turn to Jerry to give the answer. It got so bad that I started to hyperventilate before going into a meeting.

We'd be interviewed for one reason or another, and

the only quotes that showed up in the newspaper the next day were Jerry's. Now I must admit, he did have a way of speaking in quotes, but come on!

When the articles finally did come out, the first thing I looked at was the company name, because I was sure that was the only place my name would show up. Unfortunately, because the typesetting-gods were against me when the company name was spelled out, my name always ended up hyphenated at the end of the break in the copy, Trav- isano.

Not only was I the "second banana," my skin was being peeled at the same time. We were doing well, and yet I was experiencing failure.

One night late, while I was walking down the hall-way, a phone rang, which was a direct line from the type shop that we used. We did so much business with them that they put in a direct line at their own expense. So I picked up the phone, and the person on the other side of the call said, "Della Femina?"

I said firmly, "This is Travisano!"

He said, "Oh, I'm sorry. I must have called the wrong number," and hung up.

I mean, this guy had a direct line into our office for God's sake. Shouldn't he have known who I was?

Then there was the time we had this new business meeting in Philadelphia, and we decided to stay overnight for a very early presentation in the morning.

Since I lived in New Jersey, I decided to drive to Philly. Jerry Della Femina, Patrick Bohen, and Jim Travis took the train.

When I got to the hotel, I went to the front desk and asked if Mr. Della Femina had arrived yet. He said, "No, Mr. Della Femina hasn't arrived yet.

"Well, has Mr. Bohen arrived yet?"

He said, "No, Mr. Bohen has not arrived as of yet."

"Well, has Mr. Travis arrived yet?"

"No, he said, and neither has Mr. Ano."

If I hadn't been on an ego-slide into oblivion, I might have seen the humor to that.

I said to myself on the long drive home, "If I were to die in a plane crash, the headlines the next day would read … DELLA FEMINA MOURNS PARTNER!"

A week later, we had a new business meeting set up, and when it came time for me to go in and present. … I just couldn't do it. I began to gag. I was having a mini-breakdown right there in my office.

I had already been going to two private meetings a week with a shrink along with one group session, but it wasn't really doing much good.

There I sat in my office, unable to move. The experience was devastating. Frank DiGiacomo (my cousin— who was one of the copywriters) and Bob Kuperman (our creative director) sat with me, trying desperately to console me.

"Listen, Ron," Kuperman said, "I just did this thing that changed my life, and I think you should do it."

"What's that?" I asked through the gagging.

"Est!—Erhard Seminars Training!" he said. "In two weekends, you will accomplish what it will take years to accomplish with a shrink … and for a lot less money!"

Est was created by a man called Werner Erhard in the early '70s and was considered the best self-help process out there at the time. I was desperate, and after going to a guest seminar, I signed up.

There I sat in a room of about two hundred or so people, and the process of breaking down our images of ourselves, and who we thought we were, began right away.

I remember this large intimidating looking man in the front row with a shaggy looking mane and a cast on his right paw … I mean arm, from breaking a bunch of bricks in a karate class. He was doing everything but growling. He stood there towering over Randy MacNamara, the trainer, in a face-to-face standoff. Then Randy reached up and whispered something in his ear, and the lion of a man turned into a lamb right before our eyes.

Randy said, "Do you mind me telling everyone what I whispered in your ear?

"No," whimpered the sheep in lion's clothing as he melted into his seat in a gush of tears.

"All I said to him was... You're scared, aren't you?"

That blew us all away!

We went through all kinds of processes that first weekend. At one point, we were asked to imitate teapots. We had to extend one arm like a spout, while the other was tucked into our side like a handle. We then sang in unison, "I'm a little teapot short and stout. This is my handle. This is my spout. Tip me over and pour me out!"

"Again!" yelled the trainer.

"Again ... and this time say it like you mean it ... Remember ... you **are** a little teapot!"

On another occasion, we had to yell out, "Don't you ever, ever, ever let me catch you brushing that dog's teeth with my toothbrush!"

This scientific sort of thing went on and on and on, without going to the bathroom for a pee break, I might add.

In retrospect, I believe they were trying to confuse our brains to help create a whole new set of notions about ourselves different than the ones we came with.

At the end of the second weekend, after experiencing more new discoveries than Christopher Columbus, we were told that we were machines! Some people were belly-aching machines, princess machines, egotistical machines, and others were just plain old boring machines ... but machines none the less.

We discovered that we were the gods of our own universe and responsible for the way our lives had turned out so far. We could then, being responsible for the way it is, make our lives into whatever we wanted our lives to be.

On graduation night, we were given a little pamphlet as a personal gift from Werner Erhard himself entitled, "If God Had Meant Man to Fly, He Would Have Given Him Wings: or: Up to Your Ass in Aphorisms."

I may not have sprouted wings that night, but I went flying out of there with a new quest, to turn every single person I met onto this life-changing experience!

The next day I walked into Jerry's office, all puffed up and ready to share with him the new and improved Ron.

"Jerry, you need to experience this … what a trip!"

I began to quote aphorisms like a Guru on uppers, "Happiness is a function of accepting what is."

"Yeah," Jerry said as he peered over his thick glasses.

"Love is a function of communication. Health is a function of participation, and self-expression is a function of responsibility."

I had never known Jerry to be speechless before, so I was sure that what I was saying was having a real impact on him.

"And Jerry," I said in a dulcet tone.

"Yes!"

"I know that I know that I love you … and what I

want you to know … is that I know… You love me."

"Nice… What is this seminar called?" Jerry asked.

"Est! Erhard Seminars Training!" I shouted with joy!

"Sorry," Jerry said, "I believe you train dogs, not people."

Well, Jerry wasn't the only person who didn't want to hear my proselytizing. People began walking the other way when they saw me coming down the hall, but I didn't care. At least I stopped throwing up before going into new business presentations.

Nothing to Lose, and Everything to Gain

That is the way we approached all new business presentations. You had to!

If a prospective client could smell desperation in the room, there was no way he was going to turn his business over to you. The truth is it came pretty naturally to us. We were having a good time, and people want to be around people who are enjoying themselves.

New business presentations began to be fun for me now that I had a better sense of self.

Performing well and looking as though you knew what you were talking about was extremely important; however, it also set the stage for disasters to happen.

Jerry, in an effort to look suave, would light a cigarette and place it in the ashtray. Unfortunately, he was so unconscious about the act that before the meeting was over he would end up with about four cigarettes in the ashtray, all burning at the same time. One meeting, after having lit three cigarettes, I saw him groping for a fourth and unfortunately he picked up a piece of chalk and tried to light it.

One day we were given the opportunity to present to a company by the name of Knomark Manufacturing Company that produced Tidy Bowl and Esquire Shoe Polish. In the middle of the meeting, Jerry slips me this message and motions for me to read it. Knowing that he loves breaking me up in the middle of a presentation, I shook my head, no! He mouthed the words, "Read it … It's important."

I had fallen for that one before, like the time we were pitching an ice cream company, and the client said that they were a virgin company in the area of marketing. Jerry shot me a note that read, "Does this mean as a virgin company, they can't serve cherry ice cream?"

"No," I mouthed.

He repeated himself but more intensely this time. Against my better judgment, and thinking that this might be a case of him having cried wolf so many times, I opened the note. The note read, "We can package Esquire Shoe Polish and Tidy Bowl together for people who don't know shit from Shinola."

The son-of-a-bitch got me again, and I had to rush out of the room in a coughing fit.

Then there was the time Jerry was nervously tapping the table leg with his foot while he was talking, only to find out later in the meeting that it was the client's wooden leg.

When we had to take the presentation on the road, we had to bring our commercial reel with us, projector and all. This was long before the rear projection machines, the three-quarter inch tapes, the quarter-inch tapes, the CDs, DVDs, and the IUDs. We're talking slightly after the introduction of talking pictures. Just kidding!

Anyway, we were making a presentation to a man by the name of Al Kestenbaum, the marketing director for Geritol. By the time I lugged all the equipment to his office and set up the projector and screen, I could have used a shot of Geritol.

We did our presentation thing. I turned out the lights and turned on the projector. I watched with intensity his reaction to every commercial, and I must say I liked what I was seeing. Then I turned my attention to the projector. Somehow the film never connected to the take-up reel, and there in Al Kestenbaum's beautiful conference room lay a huge pile of film. It looked like Godzilla had taken a dump!

Thankfully, he remembered the work and not the presentation because we ended up working for him for years.

Then our technology took a major step forward. We went to presentations with what is called a rear-projection machine, which meant that the film was on a continuous loop. I didn't have to contend with loading the film into the projector or even have to deal with a screen. It was nicely and neatly housed in a self-contained box with a handle ... slightly lighter than a Volkswagen Bus.

In our first venture with the rear-projection machine, we were poised to present our wares to some cosmetic company. The Vice President of Marketing announced upfront that he had just quit smoking two days prior. He was so wired; he looked like he had St. Vitus' Dance. He was chewing gum and blinking his eyes as he reached out to shake my hand. I attempted to switch the projector from my right hand to my left, and I cracked him right in the knee. He went down like a sack of potatoes. For some reason, he never heard a word we said from that moment on.

Jerry and I once had a meeting with the WASP-iest potential client I had ever seen. He was from a frozen food company, which will go unnamed here. He was a rather small fellow with this tiny little vest, and he looked at us through these Coke-bottle-like glasses, which gave way to these magnified beady eyes.

He was very excited about a new product line that he was instrumental in creating and had the complete tabletop covered with the newly designed frozen food packages. He sat directly opposite Jerry and me with his little arms flailing about as he delighted himself with explaining each and every design.

Finally, he paused, staring at both of us to check out whether we were as excited as he was. He then made the fatal mistake of quickly crossing one leg over the other, bursting forth a very loud and squeaky fart. His eyes darted back and forth from Jerry to me ... and back again. Everything would have been fine if he hadn't said anything. We could have made believe we didn't hear a thing, but he couldn't leave well enough alone.

"I'm sorry," he blurted out.

I began picking up packages of frozen foods and reading them aloud, trying desperately to hold back an outburst of laughter.

"Frooozzzennnnnnn   meatbaaaalllls   Ha! Cornnnnnnn annnnd Carrrrots Hee Hee!"

The truth is, I don't even remember him leaving the room. I really believe he just sort of dissolved or went up in a puff of smoke somehow. We certainly never saw nor heard from him again.

Around the same time, a good friend of mine, Bernie Zlotnick (a successful Creative person in his own right and one of the original investors in our agency) wrote an article for Art Direction Magazine on a monthly basis. He wrote stories and satires about noted people in the business. He remembered an incident that took place during one of our new business presentations and thought it appropriate for his column. Here is the article:

"My Friend Ron"

It was a beautiful fall afternoon when I met my old friend Ron for lunch at the Burger & Brew Restaurant.

Ron and I go back 10 years to when he and I worked together as art directors at one of the hot agencies of 1963.

As I think back now, I remember Ron being sort of wild and bordering on craziness. But the agency overlooked all of this because he was one of the nicest guys and one of the best talents in the agency.

He and I were good friends, went to a diet doctor together, went to lunchtime movies, and even judged a show in Dallas.

He really was a lot of fun, but unexpectedly he would pull something wild that would throw everybody off. That's why people loved him.

In 1967, Ron, with author Jerry Della Femina, started their own advertising agency with no accounts, and today almost 7 years later, bills around $350,000,000.00. It is one of the hottest creative shops around and has been pulling in big, new business almost weekly.

"What's the secret behind your new business record?" I asked as we dove into our hamburgers.

Ron shrugged and answered, "Bern, I dunno'… It's crazy… I think it's a combination of creative and chemistry… Clients come to see us because they know they'll get good work and have fun at the same time.

"You can tell right away if you're connecting with the people across the table. You can feel it … and when you hit it

right ... it's like magic. Some people connect with my partner, and some connect with me ... or they don't connect period.
It's that simple.

"You never know for sure how you're gonna' get an
account. For instance, last week, we got this two million
dollar account through some really crazy circumstances...
So help me, this is a true story.

"It was a usual morning presentation ... held in our
well-appointed conference room where we were to present
to the Chairman, the President and two Vice Presidents of
the company.

"This particular morning, I walked into the meeting
late, and Jerry was in the middle of presenting our work.
I could feel the vibes in the room weren't too good. I could
see it in Jerry's eyes. It was going downhill fast... The suits
were sitting on the other side of the table, looking into space
and tapping their fingers on the table as though they were
counting the seconds to departure.

"I picked up a few of the ads in hopes that a new presenter
might liven them up a bit, but they continued to tap their fingers while glancing at their watches ... the way a child would
do waiting for the school bell to sound... It was murder.

"As I began to show some watch ads that we had done
in the past, they continued to go off somewhere. I was

suddenly struck with an insane idea … I had nothing to lose … The meeting was in the toilet anyway … so I stood up, closed my eyes, and shouted, 'Watches, watches! Wait, I have a vi-sion … I see two gentlemen with watches … sitting in this very room…'

"*As I continued to babble, I could see Jerry and our account people looking at me like I had gone off my rocker.*

"*I continued… 'One of you gentlemen has a watch with a soft outer coating … and you are upset because it scratches too easily, and you want to send it back to the manufacturer.'*
Well, across from me, the man's eyes opened up like two sunny-side-up eggs.

"*I went on… 'And there's another gentleman in this room who has a Pulsar watch, and he is really mad because the watch is five seconds off every day … and he's headed for a watch repair right after this meeting.'*

"*Bernie… the room went bananas!*

"*One of the guys stood up… 'How do you know this? … Is this place bugged or something?'*

"*Everybody began to laugh, and Jerry looked at me as though I had turned into Kuda Bux.*

"*I admitted to everybody that I had come in late, dressed*

in jeans and a leather jacket and rode up in the elevator with them. I went into my office, changed my clothes, and came to the meeting late. Obviously, I had heard their entire conversation in the elevator, and they didn't recognize me. They probably thought I was a messenger.

"The whole tenor of the meeting changed, and to make a long story short, we got the account.

"Jerry laughed, 'You are definitely insane.'

"Well, Bernie, that's the truth, the whole truth and nothing but the truth."

The waiter came around with the check, as I wiped the tears from my eyes and stopped laughing.

"Hey, Ron... the check!" I said. With that, Ron put his hands to his head, stood up, and said, "Check... Check... Wait, I am having a vision... I see a red-headed guy taking out his wallet..."

Another time, our accountants set up a meeting with a company in New Jersey who had just created a new biodegradable laundry detergent. Jerry and I mustered together our presentation and made our way to their offices by limo.

We were greeted by the advertising director outside the offices, which I thought a tad strange to begin with, but once inside, I began to open up the portfolio to get at our work.

"Gentlemen, there is no need to show me anything. You have the account."

I shot Jerry a look.

"Our presentation is very simple and..." Jerry tried to explain.

"I understand ... but there is no need to show me anything. You come highly recommended."

Then this swarthy looking guy comes waltzing in from another room, and the advertising director says, "I would like you to meet our marketing director..."

I shot Jerry another look... This was beginning to remind me of the court scene in the movie, *On the Waterfront*, where these gang-ridden waterfront union representatives, led by Johnny Friendly, were enumerating their job titles before the judge trying to sound business-like.

On the way back to New York, I said to Jerry, "This smells funny to me. We've never had someone give us their business before without checking out our work first ... and that marketing director, I could have sworn there was a bulge under his jacket on his left side just under his shoulder."

When we got back to the agency, I decided to run a D&B on them to see what I could find out about them. The report came back noting that the "Marketing

Director" had been indicted for murder, but was found not guilty of a man committing suicide while he was in the room.

"That's it!" I said to Jerry… "We've got to call them up and tell them we cannot take their account. We have a conflict of interest or something!"

"What's the conflict of interest?" Jerry asked me.

"My conflict is… I'm interested in living… That's what my conflict of interest is."

We called the next day and turned down the account … politely! I mean, how would it have looked for an advertising agency called Della Femina Travisano and Partners to be hooked up with Louie "The Nose" for a client.

Thank God we called it off because a few weeks later, they were all indicted for killing some supermarket buyer for not accepting an offer he couldn't refuse. I guess this was the marketing director's idea of "forced distribution."

By the Skin of Our Teeth

Jerry and I often worked as a creative team together. The clients that came to our agency wanted the people who created the original success to be working on their business. You can't blame them, but the bigger we got, the less possible that became.

I always loved working with Jerry. He was like a popcorn machine, but you had to be astute to separate the bad kernels from the good ones.

We would sit in a room and lay out what the agreed-upon positioning statement was that separated the client's product from the competition. Then we would proceed to talk about sex, restaurants, and how the Giants were doing for the next hour. We laughed away more hours than you could ever imagine … and then in whatever allotted time was left, we somehow came up with the campaign.

Just before we would have a breakthrough, I would say, "Jerry, I think we have gone too far this time," and "Whamo!" There it was.

I don't know how other teams worked, but it was the right formula for Jerry and me.

One night we were at a commercial film director's studio at around 10:30 PM, and we noticed his producer working diligently over some paperwork. On his desk was a hamburger sitting without so much as a bite out of it. I said to Jerry in an insightful poetic moment, "There is a certain amount of glory in that cold hamburger just sitting there on his desk." I mean, here was a man so engrossed in his work that he didn't even have time to take a bite out of his burger.

The next morning, Jerry and I were charged with coming up with a motivational advertisement for one of our clients, and we only had about two hours to do it.

Of course, we talked about sex, restaurants, and the Giants for the first hour, and suddenly reality struck us. The client was going to be here in one hour, and not only had we not even begun to think about the creative execution, but we would have to render a layout and write the copy in 52 minutes ... exactly!

"Jerry," I said, "This time. I mean this time, we really have gone too far."

We sat there for the next minute or two and then had the audacity to talk about the night before at the director's studio when suddenly it hit me...

"That's it!" I yelled.

"What is it!" He said desperately.

"The glory of a cold hamburger ... now there's meat for a motivational ad if I ever saw one, if you'll excuse the pun," I blurted out.

Jerry ran out of my room to write the copy, and I proceeded to draw a huge hamburger on the page with the headline, "The Glory of a Cold Hamburger."

The client loved it!

We have gone as far as to bring art pads and Magic Markers on planes, utilizing the 6-hour flight from New York to Los Angeles to make a presentation that was scheduled for that afternoon in our California office. The time change worked wonderfully with our style of creating!

We always felt that the best advertising came from real-life experiences. The trick, however, was making the real-life experience come alive when executed.

As I said before, one of our first clients was Squire Hairpieces for Men. Now, since I am still walking around with a full head of hair and Jerry lost his before he was 25, you know whose real-life experience motivated the work that was produced.

Jerry created the first advertisement for Squire Hairpieces before we started the agency, and I used it as a teaching device at Pratt Institute for twelve years. The visual was a simple one. It showed a small black comb lying in limbo with one or two hairs left in it. The headline read, "Are you still combing your memories?"

Now that is an ad I could never have envisioned because the experience wasn't one I could relate to with the mop of hair I'm walking around with. The copy went pulling at emotional hairs of the reader's head by saying things like, "...you avoid two-way mirrors." Now, I can relate, being overweight, to the concept of avoiding three-way mirrors, but not as it relates to hair.

I think everyone can relate to seeing a person wearing a bad toupee. Some of them look like they're wearing a divot from their last golf outing.

Well, with that in mind, Jerry and I came up with a real honest statement that anyone could easily relate to. I showed a photograph of a man cropped just below his eyes at the bottom of the page. He was looking up with a forlorn expression at the horrendous toupee that sat precariously on the top of his head. The headline read, "If you are going to look like a clown in a hairpiece, we'd rather you stayed bald."

The Sound of a Tom-Tom!

It was around 1973 that I received a phone call from my gay friend from Pratt Institute, Tom Parmagianni. I hadn't seen Tom for years, and it was actually great to hear from him. He wanted me to join him and his partner to visit their apartment and then go out to dinner. I said yes immediately, and as soon as I hung up the phone, I went to Mark Yustein and said, "You are coming with me for dinner whether you like it or not … I would feel a lot more comfortable!"

His lover's name was Tom also, and I was all ready to hear that his last name was Fettuccini or Baked-Ziti.

Their apartment was almost a cliché for what you'd think a gay couple's apartment would look like. They had a lot of lace and frilly stuff around, and their little Cocker Spaniel actually had a jewel-studded collar.

They showed us around their apartment, and it made me a little uncomfortable to see just one bed. Dinner wasn't very pleasant either because Tom's Tom wasn't treating me very nice at all. He kept making all these little snippy, sarcastic remarks.

Between dinner and dessert, I went to the bathroom, and while I was relieving myself, Tom (my Tom—not his Tom) came into the bathroom.

"I want to apologize for the way Tom is acting," said Tom.

"Yeah, what's that all about?" I said uncomfortably, speaking to a gay man in the bathroom while peeing ... friend or no friend.

"Well... Well, you see... He knows that I was in love with you in college."

I never heard the rest of that sentence because somewhere between an instant flashback of our naked swimming class together and the reality of his being in love with me ... I managed to pee on my pant leg.

Unfortunately, not many years later, I heard that my friend Tom was one of the first people to die from AIDS.

Raining Cats & Dogs

The Agency really began to grow by leaps and bounds. We created some incredible success stories that were based not only on powerful creative executions but on some unusual marketing strategies as well.

For Blue Nun Wine, which is a rather sweet Liebfraumilch, we took a look at the unsophisticated American market. That market had a hard time pronouncing the names of German and French wines as well as how to decide which wine to drink with what meal.

"Well sure, I know that red wine goes with meat and white wine goes with fish, but what do I drink with say ... Brussels sprouts?"

That coupled with the fact that most consumers were intimidated by the sommelier with a silver cup hanging around his neck and having to say things like Sauvignon Blanc, Pouilly Fuissé or Châteauneuf-du-Poop... I mean, Pape!

With the unsophisticated wine drinker in mind, we created a new and different positioning statement for Blue Nun!

First, to make it easy for them, we subordinated the category name of "Liebfraumilch" on the label and increased the Blue Nun brand name, which is far easier to say. Then we came up with a positioning statement that gave the consumer complete confidence by stating that

Blue Nun Wine is the wine that goes with any dish.

Sarah Bragen, Kay Cavanaugh, and Mark Yustein came up with a brilliant radio campaign utilizing the talents of Stiller and Meara (parents of the now-famous Ben Stiller) that not only won several creative awards but the hearts of consumers who were now given permission to order wine without intimidation. Now they no longer needed to wonder what wine goes with what food and no longer had to trip over a tongue-twisting name.

Sales went through the roof!

As I mentioned earlier, with Beck's Beer, we turned a brand that was importing fifty thousand cases of beer a year to a brand that was importing a million cases a year with a simple message and an even simpler media buy. With not a lot of money, we initially went from market to market, flooding them with 10-second TV commercials. As the sales grew, so did the advertising budget. One successful market allowed us to move to another and another and another.

Becoming known for our successes in the packaged goods business attracted Ralston Purina to our doors.

Initially, we were given several projects to test our abilities. We were going back and forth to St. Louis like it was a milk route.

I remember on one visit being taken to one of their storehouse facilities—it was more like a small town than a storehouse. The place was so huge that it had the trains parked inside the building, and it had streets with names like "Feline Alley" and "Doggy Lane." There was cat and dog food piled 40 feet high as far as the eye could see.

I was blown away and muttered under my breath, so I thought, "This is amazing."

The marketing manager, who was our guide for the day, snapped his head around towards me and asked, "What did you say?"

"This is amazing!"

He turned his head back toward the scene, proudly surveying it all. "Yes, it is … isn't it!"

I must have chuckled a bit as I said once again, "This **is** amazing," because his head snapped around again.

"Just what is it that you think is so amazing?" He said, trying to make sense of my chuckle.

I laughed and said, "That all of this … I mean, **all of this** … is going to end up on someone's lawn."

Although he obviously saw no humor in that comment, he feigned a smile. I guess he chalked it up to me being a creative type and that he needed to take the bad with the good.

As crazy as they thought we were, they decided to give us a project to develop a new dry cat food brand—from beginning to end. That meant we had to come up with the name, the package design, and an advertising campaign that would make its mark in a growing cat food category.

After several creative groups were asked to put their hands to the plow, so to speak, Neil Drossman and Bob Kuperman came up with a great name, a great positioning statement, and a wonderful creative. They came up with the name "Meow Mix," and the positioning statement was simply stated—"Meow Mix, the cat food that cats ask for by name."

It was brilliant, and through many award-winning creative print ads, and radio and television commercials, it became the leading dry cat food within just a few months.

I had the opportunity to get in on their successful campaign when the editor, Joe Lione, found a piece of footage with the cat chewing in such a way that it looked as though he was either singing or talking. Joe thought it would make a great commercial, and I agreed. Unfortunately, no one on the creative team wanted to do something with it, so I took a crack at it myself. We took the five or ten seconds worth of cat-chewing footage and printed it forward and backward until we had enough to fill a thirty-second commercial. Then I wrote the lyrics, "I want tuna … I want liver … I want chicken, please deliver … Now you know the cat's meow means Meow Mix, Meow Mix… meow, meow, meow!"

We employed Tom McFall to write the music and got Linda November to sing the song. We put the lyrics at the bottom of the commercial with a bouncing ball, and it became the highest-scoring commercial in after-day-recall-testing in Burke's testing history.

To this day, they are still using the same basic song—and that was more than forty-five years ago.

With that huge success story under our belts, the Ralston Purina Company decided to give us another shot at a new product in the moist cat food area.

The Meow Mix project taught us a lot, and we were feeling confident that we could repeat our success.

We put several teams together, and after months of hard work finalized on the name "Whisker Lickin's." We created several package designs and some wonderful TV commercials. We tested it and retested it, one focus group after another, listening to women slobbering over their precious little "kitty-poos."

I spent more time in dark rooms, looking through two-way mirrors, that when I emerged from those dingy closets, they would check my shadow to see if spring was coming soon.

Like Meow Mix, which is "The cat food that cats ask for by name," "Whisker Lickin's" is what cats do when they are either hungry or like the taste of what they just ate.

Finally, we went to test market with total confidence that we had rung the bell one more time … only to find out that we had bombed big time!

It was a total failure in every way, and the Ralston

people were about to descend on us as we were tripping over the tail between our legs.

What are we going to tell them? They had spent millions on this project, and when they entered the conference room, it seemed as though they were walking in extreme slow motion ... and their voices sounded like a Billy Eckstine record playing at the wrong speed.

"Weellll, geeennnttlllemmen, whaaaat ddooo youuuu havee to tellllllll us?"

I began by doing my famous imitation of Porky Pig, while Jerry was lighting cigarettes faster than a speeding bullet.

We gathered ourselves as best we could and told them that we were sorry, but the project did not meet with the standards that we had hoped for in any way.

"Gentlemen ...we have failed ... and we honestly don't see a way to turn it around without spending a fortune ... and we don't believe the numbers are worth the chance."

A deafening silence filled the room as we sat starring at them across the table.

Suddenly, two of them looked at each other and smiled, and then actually laughed a little. Jerry and I looked at each other as if to say, "Am I missing something here?"

"Gentlemen fret not. We actually accomplished what we wanted to accomplish, and that was ... keeping the competition off the shelves."

This was marketing on a level which neither Jerry nor I nor any of our highly-paid marketing people had ever even considered.

The idea that shelf space in a supermarket could be that valuable, that they were willing to spend millions on creating a product just to keep their competition off of those shelves, was incredible to us.

In their minds, they couldn't lose. If the brand had become a success, they would have applauded a new entry into the market place, and if it didn't make it, they were successful in keeping the shelf space out of the enemy's hands. Wow!

The Rich and Famous

I always found that the bigger the star, the nicer they are.

Neil Drossman and Nick Gisonde created this wonderful print campaign for Teacher's Scotch that utilized famous people talking about Teacher's Scotch in their own vernacular. Of course, their "own vernacular" was written by Neil, who was told by Groucho Marx, "You do me better than I do me."

Unfortunately, Nick Gisonde was in the hospital at the time that some of the ads needed to be photographed, so I covered for him.

One of the first ads was with George Burns. The headline read, "I love to sing. And I love to drink Scotch. Most people would rather hear me drink Scotch." We shot the photo at his home in Beverly Hills, and it looked exactly like what I remembered from his television show. You could almost hear them dialoguing in the hallways.

George: "Did the maid ever drop you on your head when you were a baby?"

Gracie: "Don't be silly, George. We couldn't afford a maid. My mother had to do it."

Gracie: "Guess what George, my sister had a brand-new baby."

George: "Boy or girl?"

Gracie: "I don't know, but I can't wait to find out if I am an aunt or an uncle."

Sorry for slipping into nostalgia. I couldn't help myself. Anyway, while we were setting up to photograph him, he took me on a tour of his home. He had one entire room turned into a wardrobe closet with literally hundreds of outfits. It was clear that he never ever threw anything away. He must have gotten that from his friend Jack Benny.

He asked me about my family, and I said that they just happen to be with me at our company home in Hollywood Hills.

"Well, tell them to come over, why don't you!" he said.

As you can imagine, that didn't take much coaxing. He was so excited to have my family there. He served them ice cream and told stories about when he was a kid swimming in the Hudson River.

"We used to swim from garbage to garbage," he said with that wonderful glint in his eyes. My son Philip had broken his arm a week before the trip, and Mr. Burns took great delight in signing his cast, which he still has.

As we left the house, I turned to wave goodbye to him as he stood in the doorway, and I could swear I heard:

George: "Say good night, Gracie."
Gracie: "Good night, Gracie."

On another occasion, I covered for Nick and Neil for an ad with Mel Brooks. This, I don't mind telling you, was one of the great thrills of my life. I went to film him the day after he had just wrapped the movie *Young Frankenstein* and he literally took me by the hand and led me through the entire set, explaining everything in detail. He was like a kid showing me the tree house that he had just built. I'll never forget it.

Mel had created a character called the 2000 Year Old Man, and Neil and Nick put together an ad that said, "2000 years ago, when you had a Scotch on the Rocks, you really had a Scotch on the Rocks."

The visual was a picture of Mel in a caveman's outfit with a stone ax sitting on a pile of rocks.

Mel loved the ad but didn't really think the caveman outfit was right. He wanted to be sitting on the pile of rocks in a high hat and tux.

I said to him, "That's not funny."

He looked at me with this strange expression.

"You know, Travisano, I do know something about humor!"

"Yes, but I know something about advertising, and this is a print ad. You aren't performing, so the picture has to speak for itself. The high hat and tux is a joke on top of a joke, and in print, it won't work."

He gave me that same strange expression again.

Like the mensch that he is, he said, "Travisano, I'll

tell you what… Let's shoot it both ways, and if you are right—I'll send you a case of scotch, and if I am right— you send me a case of scotch."

"Deal," I said.

Thank God, because I wouldn't have been able to face Neil and Nick if I had taken a dive.

Well, we shot it both ways, retouched it both ways, and sent the pictures to Mel Brooks. A week later, my secretary excitedly informed me that Mel Brooks was on the line.

"Travisano, the scotch is on its way."

That was over forty-five years ago. The ad was a success, and I am still waiting for the case of scotch.

Then there was the Redd Foxx ad. The headline for this one was, "Redd Foxx explodes 10 myths about being black." Now the visual that Nick Gisonde came up with was a picture of Redd Foxx eating a slice of watermelon.

This time Jerry Della Femina was with me, and we pulled up in front of Redd's house in a rented car with a back seat full of watermelons. As we approached the house, Jerry, the one who always likes being in the limelight, says to me, "You tell him about the watermelons."

"Why me? You're the mouth in this organization. Why should I tell him?"

"Because you're the art director." …and he laughed with that maniacal laugh that only he can do and get away with it.

Frank DiGiacomo once said, "Jerry has a Teflon personality—nothing bad ever sticks to him."

Redd Foxx couldn't have been nicer, and like George Burns, he was delighted to show us around his home, all the while being followed by this little Chihuahua with an attitude. When we got to the backyard, there were twenty or more cages with dogs in them, big dogs and small dogs, to say nothing of the ones running around doing their imitation of free-range chickens.

Redd turns to Jerry and me and says, "You see this little guy?" referring to the feisty little Chihuahua, "He's been f_ _ _ _ing this dog and f_ _ _ _ ing that dog and f_ _ _ _ ing this dog... Finally, I had to have him spaded ... excuse the expression."

I was happy to see that he was in good humor as we sat down in his study to talk about the ad.

"So what's the headline?" he questioned.

"Redd Foxx explodes 10 myths about being black," spouted Jerry with complete confidence.

"Nice, I like it. What's the visual?"

Jerry turned his head toward me in what seemed like slow motion, followed by Redd Foxx.

"Weee-aaa ... yyyou ssseee ... weeee wwoould..."

"What is it?"

"Weee we ... woo we wwoould likeee..."

Redd shoots a look back at Jerry, then back at me.

"We want a picture of you eating a piece of

watermelon." I coughed up totally out of control.

He looked at me with a stone-cold-expression… "You ain't even going see me eating a piece of canta-loupe," he said flat out.

Well, unfortunately, we ended up shooting a kind of nondescript photo of him, but somehow the ad worked anyway.

Image… Image… Image… Sometimes, the concern over image makes one act exactly the opposite of the way you want to act.

Case in point, I was creating a TV spot for Geritol around Cyd Charisse, one of the most beautiful actresses ever. We chose her because at 50 years old she still looked incredibly beautiful and healthy. We wrote a script that opened up with her saying, "I am Cyd Charisse, and I am 50 years old…"

She accepted the proposal, signed the contract, and we flew to Los Angeles. Our first meeting was at her home, where I presented the script for her to memorize for the next day's filming. She read it, sat up in her chair as though she was seeing it for the first time, and said, "I'm not going to say this!"

"Say what…?" I said, as I began to stammer in front of my client, whose glare was piercing the back of my neck.

"I am not going to say I am 50 years old!"

"But that is the premise of the whole commercial …

you agreed to say that. You signed a contract." Beads of perspiration began to appear on my upper lip.

She turned her attention toward her den and yelled out to her husband, Tony Martin, "Tony! Tony! Can you come here, please?"

Tony came sauntering into the room with an open book in one hand and adjusting his bifocals with the other. "What seems to be the problem, Cyd?" he said in a firm but gentle voice.

Ms. Charisse took off with, "They want me to say I am 50 years old ... in a TV spot ... the whole world will see ... Geritol ... I can't ... this could ruin my career ... 50 years old ... I can't say ... why would..."

Tony cut her off in mid tirade and said simply, "Listen, Cyd, if you don't want to say that, they'll just get someone else."

She looked at Tony and then at me. "Okay."

I never saw anything like it. I was willing to pay Tony anything for him to teach me how to do that!

During my years with Est, I got involved with The Hunger Project, which was an organization that came from Werner Erhard's vision. He created a new context for ending hunger and starvation in the world.

One evening, I was at a Hunger Project gathering, and I overheard a man who had just come home from Africa. He said, "If anyone could actually witness someone starving, they would want to do whatever they could to reverse the process."

I immediately had a vision of what that TV commercial was going to be. I could see it from beginning to end, as though it was already finished. I envisioned a starving child being transformed before your eyes, from starving to healthy. I saw it in an instant.

I was beyond excited and began to enlist people to help me pull it all together. The first person I spoke to was a still photographer by the name of Nick Samardge, who was looking to go into film directing. The casting of this young child would be the first and most important accomplishment, and we went weeks trying to find just the right child to fill our needs. Once again, providence moved for us. Frustrated with what we thought would be an easy task to find the right child, I had come close to giving up.

I'll never forget it, my wife and I were embroiled in a huge argument over I don't know what, and I stormed out of the house just to get away. While driving down the main street in my hometown, I remembered something Werner Erhard said to me once, "When you are frustrated or angry, put your attention toward something bigger than yourself, and clarity will replace the frustration and anger."

No sooner had I done just that, when I saw this young Indian boy with a wonderful angelic and handsome face playing in the street. I immediately pulled the car over and asked him where he lived. He lived not more than twelve blocks from my home in the WASPiest town in the entire country.

I met with his parents, explained the concept to them, and they were quick to give their approval.

"In India, where we come from, there are many who are starving, and if my son can do something that will help in any way, we are privileged to help," his father said proudly.

The very next day, we brought Shawn (the young boy) to Nick Samardge's studio and filmed a very simple full-color scene of him sitting looking directly into the camera with a sullen look on his face and then breaking into a warm smile.

When we were pleased with the short footage, we copied one single frame just before the boy broke into a smile. We made five or six black and white prints of that frame, and then I contacted a retoucher friend of mine by the name of Emilio Paccione (brother of Onofrio Paccione) to retouch each photo at a different and progressive stage of starvation. After that, we contacted Jay Gold from Editor's Gas and re-filmed those stages in black and white, dissolving from one to the other until the boy was healthy-looking. At this point, we dissolved to the live color footage whereupon he broke into a smile.

What we accomplished was watching a starving

child become healthy right before your eyes. The voice-over (Patrick O'Neil) went on to say, "The time has come on our planet to end hunger, not merely for it to be dealt with, but to end it … once and for all … forever. The Hunger Project—the end of hunger by the end of this century."

The commercial won all kinds of awards, but more importantly, it helped establish a new context—that death by starvation no longer had to be taken for granted and that it could actually end.

Part 5

"Joseph … the DeVoted"

Joe DeVoto was my friend for years, back when I was at Marschalk Adverting. And while I was doing the Advertising Agency Mogul thing, Joe became a very well-respected commercial film director. He loved actors and had a knack for getting genuine performances out of them.

One time, I took the earphones of my Walkman off my head and placed them on Joseph. You could hear the music through the glint in his eyes as Pavarotti ran the scale to high C.

"Isn't that beautiful, Ronnie? Isn't that beautiful? I love the way he does that. What power he has in that instrument. What a voice." We were listening to an aria that could blow your socks off. "What pipes he has. That's so beautiful," he said, louder and louder trying to speak over the music in his ears.

Joseph was an incredible mixture of lion, bear cub, philosopher, and child all rolled into one. He could bellow with phrases spoken from the "mountain top" and giggle like a schoolgirl in a soda shop. He was not a particularly tall man but seemed to throw a rather large shadow.

His full name was Joseph Anthony DeVoto. Most people called him Joey. I called him Joe. He came from a rough Italian neighborhood in the Bronx, and it was fairly clear that he was hewn out of so much granite, but it was also clear that there was a bit of Shakespeare, some thespian, and a lot of artist in him as well. He had a voracious appetite for the written word, the theater, film, and art. Having spent much of his time alone as a child, the movie theater became his home. And Bette Davis, because of the powerful manner in which she projected herself, became his mother.

He was a passionate man. If you asked him about his Italian heritage, he'd be quick to tell you that the Italians taught the Russians how to dance, the French how to cook, and the English how to be gentlemen. He'd say, "We know because we've been there."

On this day he was being passionate about directing a television commercial for me for AAA, the American Automobile Association. It was about a woman and her daughter who are stranded in the rain. Her car is overheating. Her daughter, dressed in a tutu, angel wings, wand, and halo, is obviously late for her ballet recital. The two are stuffed into a telephone booth calling for help to no avail. It's pouring cats and dogs, and to make matters even worse, a tow truck whizzes on by without ever seeing them. Eventually, there would be a super at the end of the commercial that would read, "Triple-A … We'll Never Leave You All Alone."

The commercial was fun to create, and Joe was doing a great job executing it. When we worked together, we were like two big kids, laughing and acting out each scene. This was work at the level of the sandbox, with all the enthusiasm and imagination of a couple of three-year-olds. In fact, I've always maintained that we didn't work for a living. We played for a living.

We were on our lunch break, and as we listened to Pavarotti and shared our love for tenors, art, and mozzarella, I began to tell him about a screenplay that I was writing. A story about a boy who is musically and artistically motivated, but unfortunately fathered by a man whose only thoughts fall somewhere between his football helmet and his shoulder pads. "If it ain't football, it ain't."

The boy's grandfather eventually comes to live with them and nurtures the artistic side of the boy, which the father was totally incapable of doing. In fact, the father was strongly against his son having anything to do with sissy things such as art and music. Just when the young man becomes comfortable having all his talents nurtured by his grandfather, his grandfather dies.

The boy, devastated, closes down his feelings, and in short, grows to become an opera singer with a beautiful voice but void of any passion.

While attending Juilliard, he is given the opportunity to study with Luciano Pavarotti himself. Through the relationship with Pavarotti, the young man's sensitivity and feelings emerge once again, and his God-given singing talents are finally realized. Touched by the memory of the boy's transformation, I was moved to tears.

"I'm sorry, Joe. I didn't mean to break up like that."

"Are you kidding?" Joe said, "That's a gift ... a gift of tears. In fact, that would be a wonderful title for your screenplay, *Gift of Tears*. Isn't that wonderful, Ronnie?"

Actually, it was wonderful. It practically captured the whole screenplay in three words.

"Ronnie, you should never be ashamed to shed tears like that. That only means you have a soft and malleable heart. God loves that in you ... Jesus loves you. Do you know that? Do you know that Jesus died for our sins and that if you believe in Him, you will not perish but have everlasting life? That's not me saying that. That's the Word of God ... God's Word."

Whoa! How did we get from me shedding a few tears, to preaching that God and Jesus love me? My eyes must have seemed to glaze over. I know that because Joe's face began to lose focus.

"That's right," Joe went on again. "Hello there! Are you listening?"

Why did he have to start with that Jesus stuff?

...just because I revealed a little of myself.

"Joe, come on now. Who are you kidding? Remember me? I know you from when you gave new meaning to the 'F' word."

As I said earlier, I first met Joe in 1963, just after

having quit my job as an art director at Marschalk advertising agency over the dispute with the creative director. I was in the middle of packing up my belongings when Joe appeared at my door.

"I'm Joe DeVoto … Where the 'F' are you going?" he asked. "I just 'F'ing got here and you're 'F'ing going? You gotta' be 'F'ing kidding me."

Now how does a man go from highlighting every phrase with the 'F' word to Jesus loves you?

He seemed to have been delivered overnight somehow. Even Federal Express would be impressed with that.

I remember him coming to my home, which was a rather large brownstone mansion with intricately carved woodwork and leaded glass windows. Joe loved the place. He just walked around shaking his head, his eyes and taste level trained from an art school background to appreciate the work that went into the hand-done filigree on the African mahogany hand-carved fireplace and the colorization in the hundred-year-old leaded glass windows.

He stepped back from the fireplace to take a more expansive look, paused, and said, "Ronnie, this is some 'F'n joint you got here. Wow!"

This is the very same tongue that now whispers sweet parables in my ear. You can easily understand my confusion with the transformation of this man's tongue.

Although this was a major change in the man, I

remained suspicious. Anyway, I'd done my own soul searching. I didn't need this Jesus stuff.

Two years of group therapy and private sessions with a shrink taught me to take responsibility for my hurt feelings over my father leaving home at the age of twelve. I did acupuncture, biofeedback, Rolfing, and was ministered to by my own Hindu Swami Herbologist. Anyway, I was born a Catholic. That surely covered everything.

No sirree, I didn't think I could learn much from a man who died on a cross some two thousand years ago and couldn't even help himself.

"In fact, Joe," I said, "I have found a savior that lives in the here and who has totally altered my life."

"Who's that?" asked Joe.

"Werner Erhard," I replied. "You know, Est, Erhard Seminars Training."

"Well, that's nice. But let me tell you about Jesus," Joe said.

"No, let me tell you about Werner Erhard. You already told me about Jesus … anyway, I told you I'm Catholic … so I've already got the best of both worlds."

Joe began to light up at this point and count-er-punched with, "Jesus is the way the truth and the life. No one gets to the Father except through Him, and that's not me talkin'—that's Jesus."

"I already know the truth … I have found it … right

here inside me. I am the god of my universe, and for the first time in my life, I feel as though I'm in charge of the way it is," I shot back.

"Ronnie, why don't you come to church with me. It's gonna' blow you away."

"I'm living in this world, and I've finally learned how to make it work for me. And you want me to listen to some mumbo jumbo written by men that weren't smart enough to know that the world was round?" Now I had him.

The battle of "my Guru versus your Guru" went on for a long time. When Joe hooked into something, he really hooked in. Unfortunately, I'm much the same way.

"And Action!"

The Agency was about 18 years old, and the next million-dollar account that came in didn't seem to hold the same excitement for me that the first million had. I don't think it was a case of being spoiled or anything, it was just … the same old same old was becoming the same old!

As a creative person, you need to be fed the opportunity to express yourself constantly. Now that the agency had become so large (with offices in New York, California, and Japan), my job was becoming more about running the business and taking care of people's needs than it was about creating advertising.

Working with Joe DeVoto got me thinking that directing might be rather exhilarating. An opportunity came up to take a shot at it when Phil Silvestri and Rita Senders created an emotionally packed campaign for WDIV-TV in Detroit. The campaign was strong and memorable, but unfortunately, the production budget was weak and forgettable.

I asked Phil and Rita if they would allow me to get my director's feet wet by directing their spots. They felt confident that I would do a good job, and the budget situation would have prevented them from getting the kind of director that they would have been pleased with, so we went for it.

Putting the package together was as exhilarating as I thought it would be. And the fact that I could draw well really helped me create shooting boards, which are the blueprints, if you will, for making sure that all the bases are covered.

I shot four commercials for them, but the one I liked best was a spot for their sportscaster, Eli Zaret. Eli had this gravelly voice and a non-conventional style of reporting. Where most reporters end up getting the same old tired stories out of the athletes like, "Well, we need to take one game at a time," Eli would do something fresh. He would pass up the tired cliché from the winner's circle and go into the loser's dressing room for a different kind of story.

The commercial I shot for them opened with a crowd working its way down a narrow smoke-filled hallway with flashbulbs lighting the way for the winning boxer. As Eli followed along with the crowd, he passed by the loser's open door. He paused for a moment, entered in, and proceeded to interview him. It was a simple but powerful spot and enhanced an already promising career for Eli.

I must tell you, directing that spot opened up all kinds of new thoughts in my head. Directing film seemed to pull together so many of the things that I liked to do.

I was always a bit of a ham, and my mom used to

yell at me for spending so much time in front of the mirror doing imitations of people.

I loved drawing and painting, so framing a scene and designing the proper lighting came naturally to me. I was always a people person, so I really enjoyed not only working with the actors, but also the crew.

Although I'm a tad embarrassed to admit it, I liked being the center of attention as well!

Not long after, Jim Weller and I created a promotional campaign for CBS-TV, which I ended up directing … and it was huge. It was too huge for my little newly formed in-house production company to put together. So we produced it through my friend Joe DeVoto's company, JOEL Productions.

Basically, the commercial was a series of unusual vignettes depicting New York City for the exciting and unique city that it is, to the tune "New York, New York"—which was to be sung by Frank Sinatra.

In fact, our first filming was to take place at the studio where Frank was going to record the soundtrack. We sat there for hours, prepped and ready to shoot when we received the message that Sinatra decided, at the last moment, that he didn't want to do it.

Not a great way to start filming your first big-budget TV campaign, but I quickly learned that as a director, you had to learn how to roll with the punches.

We stopped traffic at Columbus Circle for hours,

filmed a man walking a white goose on a leash across Third Avenue, and must have used 200 trained pigeons before the shoot was over. We were lucky enough to get Julius La Rosa to sing the theme song, and my directing juices really began to flow.

The Tuesday Team

I was privileged enough to be chosen as part of the Tuesday Team, which was a group of creative people from around the country to create an advertising campaign to re-elect Ronald Reagan in 1984. Our first meeting at the White House was interrupted with the doors to the conference room being flung open to a barrage of flashbulbs. The electricity in the room was undeniable as Ronald Reagan entered.

"I thought since you're going to advertise the soap, you ought to meet the bar," President Reagan announced with his self-deprecating sense of humor.

He went around the table, shaking hands with each member of the team. It was very exciting, to say the least.

After a week or so of strategizing from the entire team, Hal Riney came up with a simple but perfect campaign theme. "It's Morning in America," which exemplified a new beginning and a nostalgic and positive feeling about our country.

Immediately, separate teams went off to create their ideas on the best way to execute it.

Jim Weller and I created a couple of commercials that made the grade, and I got more of my "director's feet" wet filming them.

One was a series of Americana vignettes that I ended up actually filming in my hometown of Glen Ridge,

New Jersey. We filmed the fire station, the barbershop, and children running through a water sprinkler in front of a small Victorian house.

Then we did a commercial utilizing the Statue of Liberty, which was shrouded in scaffolding while she was being restored. It was a wonderful metaphor for the rebuilding of our country's image around the world. The commercial opened up with some spectacular footage of the Statue as the morning sun rose in the background

We needed to film some close-up shots of Miss Liberty's face, which meant climbing up the scaffolding on the outside of the statue. I made it up as far as her ankle when fear gripped me, and I decided to go back down, reassuring my camera crew how much I trusted them to handle the task without me.

Once at the bottom, guilt began to plague me for letting my fear get in the way of my duty, and I proceeded to make my way back up the flimsy metal scaffolding. This time I got about as high as her calf and froze as I came around a bend that had no side-railings. My hands clutched the cold metal structure, and I could not let go for the life of me. I still don't have any idea how I made my way back down.

At the end of this commercial, we wanted to use some live footage from Reagan's 1980 inauguration. So when we recorded his voice-over for the body of the commercial in the Oval Office, we asked him to read the same end lines from his speech four years earlier so that the sound would match. Without as much as looking at the old footage, he read the lines. When we went to the studio to dub in his new recording over the picture, the shot matched perfectly.

It is next to impossible to dub voices into an already filmed monologue, even when you are looking at the actual footage. It usually ends up on par with a man wearing a bad hairpiece ... you can always tell.

President Reagan nailed it, and cheers went up in the control room when we laid the soundtrack against the picture.

"Yo … How You Doin' Beloved?"

"Mr. T, Joe DeVoto is on the phone … should I put him through?"

My secretary could sometimes be a tad overprotective.

"Joseph, how ya' doin'?" I said in the most Italian street dialect I could muster up, considering that I came from a wealthy Jewish section in the otherwise Scottish town of Kearny, New Jersey. Somehow I thought I was supposed to talk to Joe in that manner.

"You wanna' go to the Isle of Capri for lunch?" Joey said. Having always fought the battle of the bulge, I needed another plate of pasta like a centipede needs another set of legs.

"Yes," I answered before my good senses could come into play.

When I arrived, Joe was sitting in the usual spot, waiters treating him like some Mafia Don.

"Yo! How ya' doin', beloved?" Joey greeted me with a warm smile.

I always said that Joey was a mixture of contrasting characters; this one sounded a lot like Rocky the priest.

"Easy with the beloved stuff," I said. "They'll think we're on a date."

"That's funny," Joey replied sarcastically.

"Joey, may I ask you a personal question?"

"Of course, beloved … You can ask me anything."

"First of all, I would appreciate you not calling me beloved in public … It kind of creeps me out."

Joey threw me one of those all-knowing angelic smiles that made me feel like a jerk for asking.

"When did all this Jesus stuff start? …'cause the Joe I've known for years…"

He cut me off mid-sentence. "I am not the same Joe!"

"You're not the same Joe… What the hell does that mean?"

"I am Born Again! I am a new creature in Christ Jesus. Old things have passed away, behold all things have become new."

"Just like that!" I said

"Yes, just like that. Jesus took my sins away by washing me in His precious and efficacious blood. That's it!"

"You have lost it, my friend … when you start talking about washing with blood and all … I'm sorry I asked. … is that the menu … could you pass me the menu?"

"Look, Ronnie. When I say I am not the same Joe, what I mean is—once I was a sinner, but now I am not. Just like that song, 'Once I was blind, but now I can see. Once I was lost, but now I've been found.'"

"Jesus found you?" I asked. "And where was it that he found you?"

"In my bed, while I was watching a Billy Graham

Crusade. Earlier in the day, I had tripped over a rolled-up carpet on my film shoot. I hurt my leg 'big time' and was lying in bed in excruciating pain."

"Don't tell me you had a miraculous healing or something!"

Joey shrugged his shoulder, gave me a blank look, and said in a monotone voice, "Why are you always stepping on my lines?"

He proceeded to continue as though I hadn't said anything.

"He was asking people to come to the podium to receive Jesus as their Lord and Savior. Then he turned and looked directly into the camera, pointed and said, "And you in the bed, come unto the saving grace of Jesus."

"I knew he was talking directly to me, and I received Jesus right there. I felt a heavy burden just lift off of me. The pain in my leg disappeared, and I began to cry uncontrollably."

"Is this some cult you've gotten yourself into? What about the washing in the blood? You didn't actually..."

He cut me off again.

"If you read the Old Testament, you'd see that God decreed that there is no remission of sin without the shedding of blood. Therefore they would take an unspotted, unblemished, perfect lamb and sacrifice it and spread its blood on the mercy seat, and that would be the payment for sin."

"How often did they do this?"

"Once a year."

"And you're sure this isn't a cult?"

"Yes."

"Sounds like a cult to me."

"Let me finish … you're stepping on my lines again."

"There's more?"

"In the New Testament, God chose His only be-gotten Son Jesus, who was without spot or blemish, to be the sacrificial lamb to be slaughtered. In other words, Jesus stood in our place, paid the price for our sins, and shed His blood. And all God asks of us is to believe in Him and receive Him as our Lord and Savior."

"And you believe all that?"

"With my whole heart… Yes!"

"So … what's good here to eat!

Joe continued to tell me about his newfound love of God right through the manicotti and gelato. Although I didn't believe a word of what he was saying, I found it interesting to listen to him, and I must admit there really did seem to be a major change in him.

"Joe," I said, trying to talk about something other than Jesus. "Tell me what made you switch from art directing to film directing."

"I always loved film… You know the story. When I was a kid, my father took off never to be seen again, and my mom was forced to work, so I spent a lot of time alone. I lived in movie theaters. I created my own family on the big screen. In my mind, Bette Davis became my mother."

"What if I told you I was thinking about becoming a director?" I said, motivated by the conversation.

"I wouldn't be surprised."

"Why?"

"Because I have always seen that in you—bursting to come out... You would be great at it. I know that!"

Crushed Vertebras &
New Beginnings

Somewhere along the line, I developed this incredible pain in my neck that radiated through my shoulder, causing my arm to tingle and my pinky finger to become numb. I couldn't get away from the pain and discomfort.

I went to chiropractors, acupuncturists, and a Swami. I tried Rolfing and all kinds of massage therapy to no avail. After trying everything and anything, I was told that I had a crushed vertebra from years ago. They said it was pinching a nerve and there wasn't much that could be done about it. Surgery was suggested, but that wasn't a sure cure either.

The doctors finally said, "Look, it is not life-threatening … you are just going to have to learn to live with it."

Not long after having been given the bad news, I needed to go to Los Angeles to cover a commercial shoot. As usual, I stayed at the Beverly Hills Hotel, which became my home away from home for years.

I don't know if the pain was getting worse or if I was just feeling it more because of the doctor's hopeless proclamation, but I was really uncomfortable.

The following morning after taking a shower, I was drying myself off while watching TV. The 700 Club with Pat Robertson was on, and I watched it with a skeptical eye.

A black man by the name of Ben Kinchlow was on,

and he was preaching a lot like my friend Joe DeVoto. He was saying things like, "Jesus died on the cross so that you can live, and by the stripes He took on his back from the smiters ... you are healed."

I wasn't really too sure what he was saying, but the word "healed" caught my ear.

He continued to preach that if you would kneel down right where you are and receive Jesus Christ as your Lord and Savior, not only would you be saved, you would be healed. Although I was skeptical, the pain in my body was beginning to talk to me.

With an attitude of "what have I got to lose," I knelt down before the TV and said what he called The Sinner's Prayer.

I repeated The Sinner's Prayer with him. I must admit, I was thinking more about healing than salvation ... when suddenly this hot lava-like sensation started in the back of my ankle, traveled up the back of my leg, up my back ... and then my neck went "pop!" It wasn't a quiet little "pop" either! I actually thought the noise was loud enough to be heard in the next room. I was startled, to say the least.

I began to move my head. The pain for the first time in years was gone. I began to move my fingers and arm ... no tingles, no pain anywhere. "Wow, what was that? What just happened to me!" I cried out.

I jumped to my feet and ran around the room,

bending and probing to see if this was just a figment of my imagination … but it wasn't … **It was gone!**

The first thing I did was call my friend Joe DeVoto. "Joe, you aren't going to believe this."

"You sound like you're flying!" Joe responded.

"I guess I am… You're not gonna' believe this…"

"You said that already… What happened?"

"I'm not sure. I was watching The 700 Club, and this black guy…"

"You mean Ben Kinchlow!"

"Yeah, that's the guy. He said a bunch of things you always say… He said if I knelt down and accepted Jesus as my Lord and Savior, not only would I be saved, but I would be healed—physically!"

"Praise God!"

"Joe, I was healed … just like that … the pain is gone … my neck popped so loud I think they may have heard it in the next room. I can't believe it!"

"Ronnie, I'll tell you what happened. You were 'born again.' Praise God! The Bible says in 2 Corinthians 5:17, 'Therefore if any man be in Christ, he is a new creature: old things are passed away; behold, all things are become new.'"

"But the doctors said I would never get over this affliction."

"Yeah, but you just received the healing power of Jesus … Jehovah Rapha … the one who healeth thee."

I couldn't believe what had just happened. Not only was I healed of this excruciating pain and numbness, but I felt as though I was walking on air. I wasn't sure what to do with what just happened to me. Other than Joe, who could I tell that wouldn't think that I was completely nuts? All I knew for sure was that the pain and numbness were gone.

From Mad Men to God Man

This born-again experience, which manifested in my physical healing, was just the beginning. Although I had been born a Catholic and had been through all the traditions from Baptism to Confirmation, I had little understanding of what the Christian faith was all about.

I knew that my physical healing was real, but as far as understanding anything meaningful about the Bible, I was clueless. I did know, however, that something more than a physical healing had taken place. I felt different somehow, and although it may sound like a cliché—the world looked cleaner, clearer, and more colorful to me!

My friend Joe DeVoto began to disciple me. He gave me my first Bible and began to send me different tracts and books to read.

I was afraid to tell anyone about what happened to me ... "born again" and miraculous healing ... they already thought me to be crazy with my proselytizing about Est.

As the days passed, there was no question in my mind that there was an incredible change within me. I wasn't sure exactly what was going on, but as I said before, colors seemed to be more brilliant, and my focus seemed more acute. This new experience seemed to give new clarity about everything in me and around me.

From the very beginning, I told Jerry, "Right now

we have nothing to lose and everything to gain. If we ever get to that place where we have everything to lose and nothing to gain, I am out of here."

This born-again experience lit a fire under me, and I began to reevaluate where I was going and what I was doing with my life.

The agency had gotten huge for those times. We had over 300 employees, offices in New York, California, and Japan, and billings of around $400 million. So much so that the next million-dollar account no longer excited me. As I said before, it wasn't because I was spoiled or anything, it just became more about handling people's problems than it was about doing great work.

Employees would beg me to enter their ads into award shows at fifty dollars a clip; they would win an award and then demand a raise. That is not a complaint mind you. That is the way it should be, but it wasn't what Jerry and I had in mind when we started the agency in 1967. We just wanted to do good advertising and do it our way!

My father always said to me, "Do what you want; do it with love, and the money will follow." I know that's true because that is exactly what Jerry and I did, and the money for sure did follow.

I also remembered something that Jerry said to me when we first got together, "In life, you either expand or you contract. There is no such thing as coasting in the middle." Well, I was definitely coasting, and I certainly wasn't expanding. So after much thought, I went to Jerry and said, "I really like directing, and before I get too old, I'd like to take a shot at it … I think it is time for me to move on."

This was an incredibly hard thing for me to even think about, let alone actually do. Here I was half owner in my own agency, and I was contemplating starting a new venture, and at 45 years old no less.

There were those who thought (once again) that I had lost my mind, and there were some that thought it was courageous. I guess it was a little of both, to tell the truth. Here I was about to give up what most people in our business wouldn't even dare to dream, and I was looking to do something else that I didn't even know would work out.

I called my cousin Frank DiGiacomo.

Frank and I were close even as children. He always looked up to me, in that I was 4 years older… that is until he turned 15 years old when in a playful wrestling match he ended up pinning me. My "Big Cousin" act went right out the window with a simple *half nelson*.

When I contemplated starting a film company, the first person I thought about doing it with was Frank. Along with him being an award-winning writer and creative person, he had a winning personality. Everyone who meets Frank loves him, and being that I was never very good socially, I thought we would make a powerful team together.

Frank, by this time, had left our agency and started his own place, specializing in marketing imported products from Italy. Frank was fairly fluent at speaking Italian and loved opportunities that were coming his way, which made me apprehensive about even calling him.

Frank and I had a long lunch, and the first question he asked was to see the commercial reel that I had put together. Although he seemed to be impressed with what he saw, what I was asking of him was not easy, and I wasn't about to hear a snap decision from him. He obviously needed to think long and hard about it.

A week or so went by and much to my surprise … he said yes! It was a huge move for both of us, but nothing ventured nothing gained as the old cliché put it.

I was leaving my relationship with Jerry Della Femina after 22 years on good terms, and Jerry was very supportive of the challenge I had taken on. He was gracious enough to allow Frank and me to use my office as Travisano DiGiacomo Films headquarters until we found a place of our own.

Saying goodbye to all of my employees was the hardest part. My office was filled with antique memorabilia, and I decided to give each person in my creative department a memento.

Before we even found an office, I was asked to do

a documentary in Zimbabwe for The Hunger Project, which I ended up writing and directing.

What a way to start! We put a small team together from all over the country. None of us had ever worked together before, but we blended together immediately as we gathered at the airport.

We had a basic thought line that promised to be very different from any other film about hunger and starvation in the world. Instead of showing starving children with distended bellies and flies on their faces designed to pull at your heartstrings, we wanted to make a motivational film that showed people fending for themselves.

The title of the film came first, *Africa the Possibility*. Right from the get-go, the film was headed in the direction of inspiring people rather than creating a sense of hopelessness and guilt.

The day we arrived, we were almost dead on our feet from the long pilgrimage from the States. As we sat in the home of one of the Save the Children counselors that were assisting us, we were told that a celebration was going on about a mile away.

I said, "Get the equipment now and let's go! … Who knows if we'll be able to capture anything like this again?" It was wonderful. We recorded the chanting, filmed the dancing, and were infused with the energy from their celebrating until the sun went down.

Everything about this trip was miraculous. Everything we needed seemed to show right before us. It was almost as though the film was creating itself. It's one of the reasons that I love the "documentary" form of telling a story so much.

In Africa, women often have to walk as many as five miles, with a bucket on their heads and a baby slung to their backs, just to get water. Then they have to walk the five miles back to their mud hut, balancing that incredibly heavy bucket without spilling it.

With that in mind, we decided to use the digging of a well as a practical symbol of a community willing and able to fend for themselves.

We found the perfect location to start the digging. Everyone took turns helping, from little children carrying stone after stone to the strong and able men who were swinging their pick-axes to a rhythmic chant they created to help energize themselves for the heavy task.

Once we had the beginning well started, we needed to find another well that was close to being finished. As I said before, everything we needed seemed to show up as we needed it. The day we went to film the success of having hit water, they actually hit water, and no one had to talk them into being excited in front of the cameras.

Then out of the woods came ten or twelve women who began to speak to us in their native language. I asked Michael Malaure, our guide, what it was that they were saying.

"They are thanking us for finding the water for them," Michael said through a huge smile.

"You mean they think we are responsible ... wow ... line them up ... get the cameras ... this is incredible ... roll sound ... roll cameras!"

While we filmed the women, Michael translated what they were saying. It was powerful!

Before we were to head home, we took a final trip to Victoria Falls as more of a respite than anything. But this miraculous venture kept revealing ideas to us! We filmed the impressive and majestic Falls, which later turned out to be a perfect metaphor for abundance at the end of the film.

The film got lots of acclaim and helped launch my career as a director.

Stepping Out Once Again

There I was again, stepping out … going where I had never gone before, wondering if I had made a huge mistake, and at the same time excited about the possibilities that were before me.

Frank and I began to search for office space and found this wonderful loft on 19th Street just off of 7th Avenue. We hired another cousin of mine, Fred Travisano, to help us design the space. We created a conference room with glass blocks separating it from the open office area. We then cordoned off one part as a supply room with floor to ceiling shelves and another for a kitchen, which left the rest of the open area for our desks and Xerox machines.

We commissioned an artist from the Set Designers union to paint a 30' x 8' mural of the Bay of Naples. You can take the boys out of Italy, but you can't take Italy out of the boys!

I was experiencing a new and deeper sense of freedom. In the agency business, you have clients who are in constant need of care and feeding—at any time, day or night! (We had one client that had the knack of showing up just a few minutes before some celebration or holiday weekend.)

No, this was different. You put a bid in to produce a commercial, and if you were awarded the spot, within a few weeks you produced, filmed, wrapped the shoot, billed it out, and moved on to your next project.

Along with all of the exciting things that go along with directing was the benefit of giving complete attention to whatever job you were working on at the time. In the agency business, I always felt like one of those performers that spins dishes on the ends of long sticks, whereby they would have to run from one spinning plate to the next to keep them all from falling to the floor.

Yes, I was really loving this new world of mine … a lot. The only negative thing about it was that you went in and out of business with each commercial shoot. There were no ongoing accounts, no monthly fees that contributed to the bottom line each month. You were either in business, or you were out of business.

Thankfully, the success of owning and running a well-known creative agency helped open some doors. I believe many people called to see my reel out of curiosity in the beginning. What kind of a nut-case leaves half ownership in one of the hottest agencies in the business to direct other people's commercials?

Although I wasn't totally sure where my new choice in life was going to take me, I had a sense that I was doing the right thing. Perhaps my recent spiritual encounter and physical healing had something to do with it.

I believe that one of the first jobs that I was given was to produce two commercials for Campbell's Soup.

One called for twelve young boys and their schoolmaster to be eating soup around a long oak table in a lofty private school. The boys were whispering something amongst each other, and the schoolmaster asked what they were talking about. One of the young men immediately stood up, inquiring as to whether the vegetable soup had "more stuff in it."

I hired Ralf Bode, an award-winning cinematographer, believing that surrounding myself with proven talent would be the smart thing to do.

We shot it in a private school somewhere in uptown Manhattan on the West Side. One of the first scenes that we shot was a dolly move, from left to right, following each boy as they whispered one to another. Ralf created a wonderful back-lit-scene, and I was getting really excited. The next shot was to be a close-up of the schoolmaster saying, "Boys, what are you whispering about?"

Well, as I was setting up the next shot, Ralf pulled me aside to inform me that going from a moving shot to a locked-off one would probably cause a problem in the editing room. I thanked him and put a little movement into the close-up of the schoolmaster. Lesson number one… Thank you, Ralf!

The second commercial for Campbell's had a female and a male police officer sitting in their police car on a cold night eating minestrone soup. The male actor, by the way, was John Turturro, in his first and last commercial before becoming one of the most talented actors in America.

I thought about making some lighting changes and went over to the head gaffer and told him what I wanted. He didn't answer me, and with a questioning look on his face, he turned to Ralf as if to say... Help!

Lesson number two. The gaffers and the grips are really part of the cinematographer's team, and even though I was the director, the change really had to come through Ralf. In other words, I should have gone to Ralf with my request. I just took it for granted that being the director, everyone obviously must report to me. Ha!

That may be what Chief Steven Spielberg has earned the right to experience, but not I, young tenderfoot that I was.

Once I learned some of the unwritten rules of production, and what a cookaloris was, I was on my way. (A cookaloris is a cutout design that when light passes through it, a patterned soft shadow effect is created.)

I loved my new incarnation as a director. I loved every aspect of it, from designing sets to dealing with performances. I loved hanging out with crews, from setting up the shoot until it was time to wrap out. Most directors leave the room and even the building when sets are being built ... not I ... I wanted to know everything that was going on ... not to control it ... I just loved the process.

I found it exciting to see the different techniques the set artists used to create the right textures or patinas. They would apply a little sand into the paint for an old wall, for example. Or they would leave a little darkened area in the corner of the linoleum where the electrical buffer couldn't get to it. Obviously, when you remove a picture from a wall where it supposedly had been hanging for a long time, it would leave a lighter area where the picture had been. I especially liked watching them create spider webs by applying this rubber cement mixture onto a spinning device, which would then throw the web into a corner of a room or between a table and chair.

Early on, we were lucky enough to be chosen to shoot several commercials for the Isuzu Impulse Turbo automobile. The campaign was centered on an actor by the name of David Leisure, who played the part of a slick car salesman by the name of "Joe Isuzu"—who had an incredible penchant for lying … about everything.

One of the commercials was a take-off on the 1931 Frankenstein movie, which happened to be one of my childhood favorites. The concept of the commercial was to take one of their trucks and one of their cars and, with one pull of the control switch, meld the two cars into one half-truck half-car design. Joe Isuzu caressed the new car crying out, "It's alive… It's alive!" And his twin assistants also melded into one body with two heads.

We copied the original set right down to the last detail—spider webs and all. We even rented some of the original props from the 1931 movie. I couldn't believe I was being paid (a lot!) for having such a great time.

The most famous commercial from that package of commercials was called "Bullet," and it won a Golden Lion at the Cannes Film Festival in 1989.

The commercial opens up with Joe Isuzu asking, "How fast is the new Isuzu Impulse Turbo? How does 950 miles per hour sound." A super then appears at the bottom of the screen, saying, "Sounds like a lie." Joe pulls out a handgun, fires a bullet downrange, jumps in his car, takes the time to fix his hair in the rearview mirror, and takes off after the bullet. There is a series of cuts showing him driving around and even over some orange cones, pulling alongside the speeding bullet, smiling, and then pulling ahead. Finally, he screeches to a halt, and in a cloud of dust looks downrange at the approaching bullet. Holding a target in his hands, he says, "Faster than a speeding..." He proceeds to hold the target in front of his face just as the bullet hits the bull's-eye. Joe removes the target from in front of his face with the bullet caught between his teeth and says, "...well, you know."

Somehow, very early in my directing career, I became known for two things: Italian images (not a surprise) and Italian food (also not a huge surprise). I have no idea how many Tuscany type kitchens I designed and had built over the years.

Frank DiGiacomo and I were brought up with a deep and rich love for Italy, and it just so happens that the Italian ad agencies were enamored with American directors, especially with ones whose names ended with a vowel.

Without a lot of trouble, we connected up with a few Italian production companies and began filming all over Italy. I was a reasonably easy sell over there, not only for my commercial reel but because of my past agency experience and reputation. Frank and I originally just wanted to work there because it was our heritage, but we found it to be a wonderful source of quality work and income as well.

One of my favorite experiences was a commercial for Citterio Prosciutto and Salami. We worked for a well-known award-winning art director named Alberto Biccari, who had created a montage of scenes for a party that was originally supposed to be a thirty-second commercial, which turned out to be a sixty as well.

Thankfully Alberto allowed us to kind of free-wheel ideas as they seemed to show up, and we ended up with an exciting, beautifully shot piece of film.

We filmed it in the famous Italian film director Luchino Visconti's mansion on Lake Como. I remember my cinematographer Tom Olgerson and myself standing on the balcony of the mansion doing a tech scout. We were waiting to see where and what time the sun would be breaking over the hill across the lake when a servant came out with a silver tray with fresh buns and espresso coffee for us. I looked at Tom and said, "Filming in Italy is a tough job, but somebody has to do it."

Everything in Italy is a little different, to say the least. Tom decided that we needed two arc lights to produce the lighting effects we were looking for. The Italian line producer said, "We don't have any arc lights here in Milan ... we're going to have to bring them in from Rome." Well, the arc lights managed to get there in time. Unfortunately, one of them was broken.

Tom said, "But I needed two arc lights."

"You have two arc lights," the producer said confidently.

"But one of them is broken!" repeated Tom.

The producer shrugged his shoulders, doing a perfect imitation of Marcello Mastroianni from one of his bumbling roles ... as if to say, "Ah, what can we do?"

I filmed quite a few commercials shot in Italy for German clients. I found it interesting that within my own memory, this could have ever happened. I had an American producer, an Italian cameraman, a Jewish assistant, an Italian crew, and German clients. What made things even more interesting—we were filming in a little Medieval village that had been occupied by the

Germans in World War II. There was a huge wall sculpture in the town square. I found my German clients fascinated with it, and they asked me what it represented. With my heart in my mouth, I had to let them know that it was a memorial created to honor all the men in the village that had been lined up against the wall and shot by German soldiers. It was an awkward moment, to say the least, as they just shook their heads in acknowledgment and moved on.

On another occasion, I was filming in Japan with a German cinematographer, a Jewish producer, and little ol' Italian-American me. We had all of the Axis powers represented, along with the persecuted. To make matters worse, we were filming at the base of Mount Fuji on December 7th. Frank turned to me and said, "Do you know what day this is?" Those words weren't out of his mouth but for a few seconds, when all of a sudden, the sky became blackened with helicopters, and the ground covered with trucks, tanks, and hundreds of soldiers firing their weapons in our direction. What we didn't realize was that we were filming just outside of their army training grounds. What are the chances?

The Truth Shall Set You Free

My faith and knowledge of God's Word was becoming the most important aspect of my life. I was beginning to see that God had a plan for me, utilizing the talents that had been given me from birth. Starting my own agency gave me some business smarts, a creative reputation, along with communication skills, and now the film business was honing me in the area of telling an even larger story... a Christian film.

I was filming some commercials in Ocean Grove, New Jersey for Folgers Coffee, and the *Asbury Park Press* sent a reporter to do a story on me. While being interviewed, I happened to mention that I would like to use my film knowledge to do a full-length Christian-based feature film.

At the same time, my friend Joe DeVoto, who had been going to this church called Shore Christian Center, wanted me to meet his pastor, Dewey Friedel.

One of the elders of that very church had read the article about this commercial director who wanted to do Christian films and immediately called the pastor. He was excited about the article because he was convinced that this was an answer to prayer and that they should try to contact him. Pastor Dewey Friedel said on the phone, "You'll never believe who is sitting in my office right now."

That was the beginning of a long relationship with Elder Joe Raspanti, and we have since written two screenplays and filmed several documentaries together.

I could see God's hand, not only connecting me to Joe Raspanti, but my entire life walk was getting me prepared to do His will through film. One of the first projects that Joe and I were asked to do was a documentary on an aging Pastor by the name of Ern Baxter. What a blessing to be asked to film him. He was known as the Pastor's Pastor and was respected throughout the Christian world for his wisdom and knowledge. Unbeknownst to us, it turned out to be some of his last words before going home to be with the Lord.

One of the most powerful things that he said while filming him has stuck in my heart and mind ever since. He said, "I live to become, at every moment of existence, the active agent of the Divine will."

"The active agent of the Divine will."—what an inspired Word, right from the throne room of God!

In all my professional creative years in the advertising business, I thought that power, I mean real power, came to those with important titles and untold finances, only to find out that there is no higher office, nothing more powerful, than that of being a "servant."

The notion that someday I will stand before the Lord hoping to hear Him say, "Well done, my good and faithful servant," brings me to tears every time.

I have learned that Christianity, for me, is not a religion but a relationship. Praying no longer is a burden or a sacrifice; it's an incredible opportunity to fellowship with the Creator of the universe.

I know that may sound as though I have taken leave of my senses, and perhaps in some way I have.

The sense realm for me is no longer just that which I can see or touch... I have learned to walk by faith and not necessarily by sight. The Bible says in Hebrews 11:1, "Now faith is the substance of things hoped for, the evidence of things not seen."

Someone once said, "Faith in action is victory ... and that faith sees it before it happens."

I truly believe that with all my heart, and even before I knew the Lord, I was walking by that concept.

It was present when Jerry Della Femina and I set out to create an advertising agency with little knowledge, no meaningful contacts, and very little money. We held the idea of "creating a successful ad agency" in the context that it was a done deal, and all we had to do was play it all out.

Now I say, "Amen to that."

Jesus Wept

Around twelve years went by, and my directing career was doing very well. Blessed, once again—far more than I ever deserved.

I was asked to shoot a couple of commercials in California for Kentucky Fried Chicken, which was becoming a very good account for me. Whenever I filmed in LA, I tended to work with the same crew—the same wardrobe people, hairstylists, etc.

I arrived in LA Friday afternoon and went right into a production meeting with my crew. Everyone was in place except for the prop person; he was busy on another job. They introduced me to this young Hispanic man and asked if I minded working with someone that I had never worked with before. He came highly recommended, and I was quick to say that I had no problem. That was Friday night…

On Sunday I always go to church, either at Frederick Price's or Hal Lindsey's church. (I became good friends with Hal, and on a couple of occasions had the opportunity to cook for him at his house. He loves Italian food.)

Anyway, during the service, Hal was talking about how silver and gold become purified when put through fire. This was around 1995, and there were some horrendous fires devouring much of the Malibu hillsides. Hal mentioned the fires to make a point about the silver and gold being purified. He had a woman friend whose home was burned completely down and all that was left was some purified melted gold and silver.

At the same time, while using this real-life example to everyone, he also mentioned that his friend's daughter and son-in-law had a barn in the hills as well, that burned to the ground. Unfortunately, they had to let their horses go and were not to be found again for a couple of weeks in a park somewhere.

The teaching moved me, and as I was leaving the church, I glanced over at a table where Hal usually sells some of his books, and the quiet voice within me said to buy *The Late Great Planet Earth* and give it to someone.

When I experience the Spirit of the Lord speaking to me, I am quick to respond, no matter how strange it may seem, and I bought the book.

The next morning I was in my hotel room studying the Word of God and came upon the shortest verse in the Bible, "Jesus wept." It was referring to Jesus standing before the tomb of his dead friend Lazarus. When I read that, I began to cry uncontrollably. Somehow I got in touch the humanness of Jesus. He was a man like me with tears—like me, and I began to cry out to Him. "Lord, please show me some sign that all this studying I am doing is not in vain. I can't see You or touch You, and I need to hear from You."

Those words were not out of my mouth but for five

seconds when the phone rang. It was the new prop person who was calling to show me some Polaroids of some props that he wanted me to approve of. I told him to come up right away, and as I hung up the phone, I heard the Spirit of the Lord say to me, "Tell him about Me and give him the book."

Right then and there, I began to argue with the Lord, "Please, Lord. He's probably Catholic, and he won't understand about eschatology..." Before I could say anymore, there was a knock at the door.

I opened the door and invited him in, and as though I had no control over what I was going to say, I said, "Do you know Jesus?"

He said, "Oh, yes... But my mother-in-law really knows Jesus."

"Really?" I asked, "What church does she go to?"

"Hal Lindsey's Church ... Do you know of him?"

"Wow... Hal is a good friend of mine. I cook for him at his house and..."

"To show you how good a friend she is to Hal, her house just burned down..."

Now it is hitting me ... I had just cried out to the Lord for a sign, and my legs became weak beneath me.

I finished, "...and the place burned down, and all they found was the purified gold and silver?"

"How did you know that?" he said.

Now I am really beginning to sweat.

"Yeah, and my wife and I had a barn up there…"

"…and it burned down, and you had to let the horses go and didn't find them for two weeks in a park?"

"How did you know that?" he said as though he was talking to some strange soothsayer.

I am now trying desperately not to faint…

"Did you ever read any of Hal Lindsey's books?"

"To be honest with you, I have always wanted to read *The Late Great Planet Earth* but was too shy to ask him."

By now, I am absolutely shaking. I reached over to the book and gave it to him, "The Lord told me to give this to you!"

Whenever my faith gets weak or whenever I need to be reassured about my walk with God, I think about this incredible answer to prayer. The odds of that young man being who Hal had been talking about less than 24 hours earlier is mind-blowing … staggering, to say the least.

The Bible says in Isaiah 40:31, "But they that wait upon the Lord shall renew their strength; they shall mount up with wings as an eagle; they shall run, and not be weary, and they shall walk, and not faint." Amen!

To Whom Much is Given ...
Much is Required

Yes... To whom much has been given, much is required. When I was involved with New Age philosophy, I believed that I was the god of my universe, and if I created it the way it was, then I could create it differently.

There were no rules for me to follow. I could create my own rules, and it is that very outlook that has this world going to hell in a hand-basket at an astonishingly fast pace.

Everything that I was living by was exactly the opposite of what Jesus teaches. I thought that I would be judged successful or not by the amount of "toys" I ended up with, only to learn that the meek shall inherit the earth, and humble will be lifted up.

It really is better to give than to receive.

In early 2001, I officially shut down Travisano DiGiacomo Films, and in effect, retired from the commercial world. I was getting older, and the clients were getting younger. The business was turning out new young directors like jellybeans, and each week the ad world wanted to know what the new flavor of the week was.

I thought I was retiring, but my wife thought otherwise. She said, "You're not retired... You're rewired."

She was right. I found myself teaching advertising design and concept at Pratt Institute once a week. I began teaching Bible classes at my home twice a month. I taught Discipleship Training at my church, as well as a Firm Foundation course. I taught Bible classes to Renovation House for drug and alcohol abuse. I still paint. I cook. I do woodcarving. I have written, along with my partner Joe Raspanti, two Christian screenplays. I play golf—badly. And I even found time to learn how to play the piano. Oh, and I just published my memoir, in case you hadn't noticed.

Walking By Faith …
Not By Sight

The Word of God tells us that without faith, it is impossible to please God. It also says in 2 Corinthians 5:7, "For we walk by faith, not by sight."

As opposed to what I had learned in the New Age realm, Christianity is a faith walk, and I needed to learn how to walk by faith, die to self and live unto Jesus.

Over the last 10 or so years I have taught over a hundred Bible classes at Renovation House to men suffering from drug and alcohol abuse… I can truthfully say the experience of seeing these men turn themselves around has been the most rewarding thing I have ever had the privilege to do.

Jesus said that in the world we would have trials and tribulations, but He also said for us to be of good cheer, for He has overcome the world… therefore I keep my eyes fixed on Jesus, the author and finisher of my faith!

35905059R00156